REVOLUTIONARY
HEROES

REVOLUTIONARY
HEROES

TRUE STORIES OF COURAGE FROM AMERICA'S FIGHT FOR INDEPENDENCE

PAT WILLIAMS
WITH JIM DENNEY

Revell

a division of Baker Publishing Group
Grand Rapids, Michigan

Published by Revell
a division of Baker Publishing Group
Grand Rapids, Michigan
www.revellbooks.com

Printed in the United States of America

Library of Congress Cataloging-in-Publication Data
Names: Williams, Pat, 1940– author. | Denney, Jim, 1953– author.
Title: Revolutionary heroes : true stories of courage from America's fight for independence / Pat Williams, with Jim Denney.
Other titles: True stories of courage from America's fight for independence
Description: Grand Rapids, MI : Revell, a division of Baker Publishing Group, [2023] | Includes bibliographical references. | Audience: Ages 9–12 | Audience: Grades 4–6
Identifiers: LCCN 2022032654 | ISBN 9780800743055 (paperback) | ISBN 9780800744694 | ISBN 9781493441457 (ebook)
Subjects: LCSH: United States—History—Revolution, 1775–1783—Influence—Juvenile literature. | United States—Politics and government—1775–1783—Juvenile literature. | Founding Fathers of the United States—Biography—Juvenile literature. | United States—History—Revolution, 1775–1783—Women—Biography—Juvenile literature. | United States—History—Revolution, 1775–1783—Biography—Juvenile literature.
Classification: LCC E206 .W69 2021 | DDC 973.3092/2—dc23/eng/20220708
LC record available at https://lccn.loc.gov/2022032654

Baker Publishing Group publications use paper produced from sustainable forestry practices and post-consumer waste whenever possible.

23 24 25 26 27 28 29   7 6 5 4 3 2 1

This book is dedicated to *you*
and to all young freedom-loving heroes everywhere.

Contents

1

The First Shots Fired in the Revolution

Bostonians Reading the Stamp Act by James Henry Stark

There are some who say that the American Revolutionary War began with an incident involving an eleven-year-old boy named Christopher Seider. Others say the Revolution began with a confrontation between a British soldier and a thirteen-year-old boy named Edward Garrick. Still others say the Revolution began with the heroic actions of a young Black man named Crispus Attucks.

It's an exciting story—a story you'll want to tell all your friends. I'll tell you the facts, and *you* can decide when the Revolution *really* began.

The American Revolutionary War was fought between Great Britain and the Thirteen Colonies in North America from 1775 to 1787. The Thirteen Colonies were the New England colonies of Massachusetts, New Hampshire, Rhode Island, and Connecticut; the middle colonies of New York, New Jersey, Pennsylvania, and Delaware; and the southern colonies of Virginia, Maryland, North Carolina, South Carolina, and Georgia.

After years of being oppressed by the government of King George III of Great Britain, many people in the Thirteen Colonies had finally had enough. They were tired of being heavily taxed and ordered around by a government more than three thousand miles away.

In 1765, the British government passed a law called the Stamp Act. The law required the people in the Thirteen Colonies to pay a tax on legal papers, magazines, news-papers, and playing cards. The king would use the money to repay Britain's huge debts from the Seven Years' War against France (1756–1763).

Though some colonists were loyal to the king, many colo-nists rebelled against the king and refused to pay the tax. These colonists rose up and demanded the freedom to elect their own leaders and make their own laws.

Angered by the disobedience of the colonists, King George sent warships to America. In May 1768, the huge fifty-gun warship HMS *Romney* sailed into Boston Harbor, and the captain of the ship sent his men ashore to force Americans to join the British navy. The Boston colonists were furious, and they protested against Great Britain.

A few months later, in October 1768, the king sent British soldiers to America to stop the protests. The British soldiers wore bright red uniforms, so the American colonists mocked them, calling them "Redcoats."

The Tragic Death of Christopher Seider

The arrival of the British forces divided the colonies, causing the colonists to choose sides. Those who rebelled against British rule called themselves Patriots. The colonists who supported the British king and government called themselves Loyalists. The Patriots and Loyalists sometimes argued and fought with each other.

On February 22, 1770, an angry crowd of Patriots gathered in front of a Boston shop owned by a Loyalist. They shouted and threw rocks at the store. Soon, a Loyalist neighbor of the shopkeeper arrived, a man named Ebenezer Richardson. He raised a gun and told the crowd to leave.

The Patriots turned their anger against Ebenezer Richardson and began throwing rocks at his house. One of the rocks broke a window and injured Richardson's wife. Afraid for himself and his wife, Richardson fired into the crowd.

The bullet hit eleven-year-old boy Christopher Seider in the arm and chest. The boy fell to the ground and died later that night.

Hundreds of angry Patriots attended Christopher's funeral, and the *Boston Gazette* ran stories that inflamed the anger of the colonists. Many Patriots confronted British soldiers, mocking and taunting them. They blamed King George and the British government for the boy's death. The people of Boston knew that it was just a matter of time before more violence erupted.

The Incident at the Custom House

On the evening of March 5, 1770, a British soldier stood guard in front of the Boston Custom House on King Street. It was the building where British officials collected taxes on tea and other goods imported from Great Britain. The streets were blanketed with snow. The soldier shivered in the cold.

A thirteen-year-old boy, a wigmaker's apprentice named Edward Garrick, walked down King Street near the Custom House, along with several of his young friends. He saw a British captain walking by and recognized him as a customer of John Piemont, the wigmaker Garrick worked for. (In those days, wealthy men wore wigs powdered with white starch and scented with lavender oil.)

The boy shouted to his friends, "There goes the fellow who won't pay my master for dressing his hair!" The captain pretended not to hear and kept walking.

The soldier in front of the Custom House heard the boy insulting the British captain and came running with his musket in his hand. "The captain is an honorable man who pays his debts!" the soldier said.

Young Garrick shouted again, insulting both the captain and the soldier. Enraged, the soldier swung the butt of his musket, hitting young Garrick in the head and knocking him to the snow.

People saw the soldier strike Garrick, and they rushed over to help the boy. Garrick was not badly hurt, and people helped him to his feet.

The crowd turned to confront the soldier, shouting insults and throwing snowballs. The soldier retreated to the steps of the Custom House, where he loaded his musket.

The shouts of the crowd and a ringing church bell drew more people out of nearby shops and houses. A mob of more than fifty people closed in on the soldier. Fearing for his life, the soldier shouted for help.

Crispus Attucks: The First Hero of the Revolution

A few blocks away, Captain Thomas Preston heard that people were rioting in front of the Custom House. He assembled a squad of seven soldiers. By the time he and his soldiers reached the Custom House, there were several hundred people in the street, shouting insults, throwing snowballs, and waving clubs.

Captain Preston ordered his men to move the townspeople back, using their bayonets as a warning. He didn't want anyone to get hurt, so his soldiers' muskets were not loaded.

In the crowd was a Black man named Crispus Attucks. He was born a slave but had escaped to freedom. He worked as a rope-maker and a sailor. He didn't

Crispus Attucks, artist unknown

13

like the British government, and he worried that the British might capture him and force him to serve in the British navy. So he brought some sailor friends from the waterfront, and they pushed their way to the front of the crowd.

There, Crispus Attucks and his friends confronted Captain Thomas Preston with his squad of seven soldiers. Attucks faced the line of soldiers, waving his club and shouting insults at them.

Captain Preston didn't want to have to shoot anyone, but he could see that the mob was not afraid of his soldiers' bayonets. He ordered his men to load their muskets, hoping the threat of loaded guns would persuade the mob to leave.

As the soldiers loaded their guns, Crispus Attucks shouted to the crowd, "Be not afraid! They dare not fire!"

Others in the crowd took up the chant, "The wretches dare not fire!"

The mob threw snowballs at the soldiers and pressed in on them until their faces were inches from the bayonet blades. Some men batted at the bayonets with their clubs.

Crispus Attucks reached out with his left hand and grabbed the bayonet of Captain Preston's musket. At the same time, one of Attucks's friends threw his wooden club at a soldier, knocking him down.

The soldier scrambled back to his feet and fired into the air as a warning shot—but his frightened fellow soldiers thought it was a signal to begin shooting. The roar and smoke of gunfire filled the air as the soldiers fired into the crowd.

Crispus Attucks was the first man shot, hit twice in the chest. He fell to the snow.

The Boston Massacre

Captain Preston shouted to his men to stop shooting, but the soldiers couldn't hear him over the gunfire. The shooting continued.

When the captain finally got his soldiers to stop firing, eleven Boston citizens lay on the snowy ground. Three were dead, including Crispus Attucks. A fourth, seventeen-year-old ivory carver Samuel Maverick, would die the next morning. A fifth, Irish-born American Patrick Carr, would die of his wounds two weeks later. Six men would live, though one was crippled for life.

The soldiers reloaded, fearing that the mob would come at them again. Captain Preston ordered his soldiers to hold their fire. Many of the colonists fled, but some remained to care for the wounded.

Reports of the shooting spread quickly throughout the Thirteen Colonies. Patriots who already hated British rule, with its heavy taxation and forcing sailors into the British navy, were enraged at the killings in Boston. Boston newspaperman Samuel Adams gave the incident a name that would never be forgotten: the Boston Massacre.

As a Black American who was the first to die in the Revolution, Crispus Attucks became a legend among Black Americans during the era of slavery before the Civil War. His name also became a rallying cry during the Civil Rights era of the 1950s and 1960s. He died while fighting injustice in Boston in 1770—and his name continued to inspire people to fight against injustice for years to come.

Angry colonists continued to shout insults at British soldiers—and the soldiers sometimes got into fights with the colonists. British officials in the colonies realized they were losing control of the people, and they asked Great Britain to send more troops to maintain order.

2

Young Heroes in a Time of War

The Arrest of Emily Geiger by Benson John Lossing

Life was often harsh for young people growing up in the American colonies in the 1770s. Many young people left school as early as age twelve or thirteen to work on the farm or work as an apprentice to a shopkeeper or blacksmith. Those who continued in school had to study hard and learn to speak and read several languages.

In the early 1770s, Patriots formed military groups called militias. Though most soldiers were teenagers or older, some militias trained children as young as ten years old. Many young people fought in the Revolutionary War and became heroes in the cause of liberty.

Both girls and boys played a role in the cause of American liberty. Some played a direct role by spying or carrying secret messages. Others managed homes, shops, and farms to free their fathers and older brothers to fight in the war. Young ladies sewed and mended tents, flags, and military uniforms for the soldiers.

Here are a few young people who took part in America's fight for independence.

Andrew Jackson: Battlefield Messenger and Future President

When the Boston Massacre took place, Andrew Jackson was not quite three years old. He was nine years old on the day the Declaration of Independence was signed. By the time he turned thirteen, he was deeply involved in the fight for freedom by serving as a Patriot courier, carrying secret messages to American officers on the front lines.

Andrew Jackson's parents and two older brothers, Hugh and Robert, came from Ireland and settled in the Waxhaws region along the border between North Carolina and South Carolina. His father died in a tree-cutting accident in 1767, three weeks before Andrew was born. His mother, Elizabeth, wanted him to become a minister, but her hopes were dashed by his many fistfights and the mean pranks he played on his brothers and friends.

In his early years, Andrew had little idea that the Revolutionary War was going on. But by 1778, when Andrew was eleven, war had come to the Carolinas—and it had a crushing impact on Andrew's life. He saw many of his friends and neighbors join the army and march off to war, only to return crippled. Some didn't return at all.

In June 1779, his oldest brother, Hugh, fought in the Battle of Stono Ferry, near Charleston. He died of heat stroke because of the stress of battle in the hot, humid weather. After Hugh's death, Andrew's mother urged Andrew and his remaining brother, Robert, to join the Patriot cause. So they joined a local militia.

The Jackson brothers studied military tactics and practiced marching and sharpshooting with the other militiamen. Because they were too young for battlefield service, their commanding officer had them deliver messages to the battlefield.

At the Battle of Hanging Rock on August 6, 1780, Andrew and Robert carried messages between military units across the battlefield, helping to coordinate the attack of the American forces against the British. The Battle of Hanging Rock was a major victory for the Americans. Young Andrew Jackson was unafraid of the dangers of war, though he saw many soldiers of both armies wounded or dying.

The British became aware of the role the Jackson brothers played in the war effort. In April 1781, during a raid through the Waxhaws region, British soldiers burst into the home of Andrew's uncle James Crawford—where they recognized Andrew and Robert. They arrested the boys and marched them forty miles to a prisoner of war camp at Camden, South Carolina.

While Andrew and Robert were held prisoner, a British officer ordered Andrew to clean his muddy boots. Andrew sneered, "I am a prisoner of war, not your servant."

Enraged, the officer drew his saber and aimed a smashing blow at the boy's head. Andrew put up his hand as the officer struck at him twice with the saber. The first blow slashed Andrew's hand; the second left a bloody gash in the side of his head. He would carry the scars of those wounds for the rest of his life.

The officer turned to Andrew's brother, Robert, and told him to clean the boots. Robert refused. The officer struck Robert in the head with his saber. Robert fell and was unable to stand for several minutes.

In the British camp, the brothers received little food and were often treated cruelly. They came down with smallpox—a terrible disease that causes fever, vomiting, blistering skin, and often death. Their mother, Elizabeth, begged for their release. The British agreed to let the boys go.

Andrew and Robert were still suffering from smallpox when they walked forty miles to their home. Soon after they arrived, Robert died from the disease and from the injury caused by the British officer's saber.

Elizabeth cared for Andrew and prayed for him. He came close to death and later recalled that the illness had left him "a skeleton—not quite six feet long and a little over six inches thick."

As soon as Elizabeth was sure that Andrew would live, she left home and went to Charleston to care for sick and wounded soldiers. There she came down with cholera, a severe intestinal disease. She died in November 1781. Andrew was fourteen years old and had lost his entire family.

After the war, Andrew continued his education and became a lawyer. He went through many hardships, and he grew up with many character flaws. He had a violent temper, and he fought several duels (a duel is when two people fight with swords or pistols, usually to the death). He also engaged in buying and owning people as slaves to work on his Tennessee cotton plantation, the Hermitage. Slavery is a cruel practice that treats people as if they are nothing but property to be bought and sold. Slavery was outlawed in the United States in 1865, after the American Civil War.

Andrew Jackson gained fame as a general in the United States Army during the War of 1812 and served two consecutive terms as president of the United States from 1829 to 1837. He was a deeply flawed man, but as a boy, he played a part in the fight to free the American people from British rule.

Austin Dabney: From Slave to War Hero

As a Black child living in slavery in Georgia, Austin Dabney heard little about the Revolutionary War until 1779, when the war changed his life. He was fourteen years old at the time.

The cowardly slave master who owned Austin, a rich plantation owner named Richard Aycock, was called up to serve in the militia. But Aycock didn't want to be a soldier, and he was bad at soldiering. He went to his captain and offered to have young Austin take his place in the militia. The militia had rules against slaves serving in combat, so Aycock lied and told the captain that Austin was born free and wasn't a slave at all. The captain agreed to accept Austin in the man's place.

When Austin reported for duty, he had no last name, so the captain gave him the last name Dabney. The young man proved to be a brave and disciplined soldier in battle. He served as an artilleryman under Colonel Elijah Clark in the Battle of Kettle Creek on February 14, 1779. Historians believe he was the only Black soldier on the battlefield that day. The victorious American troops forced the Redcoats into retreat and broke British control of Georgia.

During the battle, Austin Dabney was severely wounded when he was shot in the thigh. The wound left him disabled for life and unable to continue serving in the militia. His fellow soldiers took him to the nearby farm of Giles Harris. As Harris took care of Austin, the two men became good friends. After his recovery, Austin stayed on the farm and helped the Harris family with their chores.

Though Richard Aycock still owned Austin Dabney, according to the slave laws of that time, he let Austin live with the Harris family. In 1786, the Georgia legislature set Austin free and gave him a monthly pension payment in thanks for his service in the Revolutionary War. The state also gave him fifty acres of land on which he raised racehorses.

When Austin Dabney died in 1830, he was buried in the Harris family cemetery. The words on his gravestone read, "Austin Dabney, c. 1765–1830, Georgia Militia, Revolutionary War, Freed Slave, Devoted Friend to Harris Family."

Emily Geiger: Midnight Messenger

In the summer of 1781, the Americans were trying to push the British out of South Carolina. American General

Nathanael Greene had spent a month trying to capture the British-held fort at Ninety Six, South Carolina, but without success. (In case you're wondering, no one knows why the town was named Ninety Six.) When Greene learned that the British General Lord Francis Rawdon was coming with fresh troops, he knew he would have to retreat.

But Greene also knew that, just seventy miles away, American General Thomas Sumter commanded a large number of troops. If Greene's troops could join forces with Sumter's troops, Rawdon's Redcoats could be beaten. But how could Greene get a message to General Sumter?

General Greene's own men were exhausted and hungry due to lack of supplies. He couldn't ask one of them to make the journey. Greene explained the situation to a Patriot farmer named John Geiger. As the two men spoke, Geiger's eighteen-year-old daughter Emily listened from the hallway. She loved America, and she wanted to push the British out of South Carolina.

After General Greene left, Emily quietly slipped out of the house and made her way to the American camp. She demanded to speak to General Greene. A soldier took her to Greene's tent, where Emily offered to take the message to General Sumter.

At first, General Greene said no. But Emily said she knew the road well, having made the trip many times with her father—and she wasn't afraid. Finally, Greene agreed. He wrote the message to Sumter on a sheet of paper, handed it to Emily, and wished her good luck.

When Emily set off on horseback, she was observed by a Loyalist spy. The spy told the British that a young lady had left General Greene's camp on an unknown mission. The British knew they should be on the lookout for her.

That night, Emily stopped to rest at a house along the road. The people in the house were strangers, but they welcomed her to stay for the night. Emily didn't know they were Loyalists, and they were suspicious of this young lady riding alone at night.

An hour or two after Emily arrived, a man came to the door. He was a Loyalist, and he had tracked Emily from Greene's camp to the house. The people told him that the girl was asleep. They invited him to rest for a few hours, and he could arrest Emily in the morning.

Emily overheard the whispers and knew she was in trouble. She waited until the house was quiet, then climbed out the window, untied her horse, and escaped. She rode hard, hoping to get far away from the man who had tracked her.

After hours of riding, Emily saw trouble ahead: three British soldiers blocking the road. They asked her why she was traveling alone. Emily couldn't come up with any good answers, so the soldiers arrested her and took her to a British military camp.

At the camp she was taken to the headquarters of General Lord Francis Rawdon himself. Hidden inside her clothes was the message from Greene, spelling out a plan for the defeat of Rawdon. If the British discovered that piece of paper, she would go to prison—or worse, be hanged as a spy.

Rawdon questioned Emily intensely: Where was she going? What was her mission? Who had sent her?

Emily knew that her nervousness showed—and that Rawdon suspected her of being a Patriot spy. He ordered that

Emily be jailed in the guardhouse, and he told her he would send a woman to search her.

The soldiers marched Emily to the guardhouse and locked her inside. She knew that a search would reveal the paper with General Greene's message. So she reached into her clothing, pulled out the paper, and began memorizing the message. Once she was sure she had memorized every word, she tore the paper into pieces—and she ate the paper.

Emily had just finished swallowing the last piece of paper when the cell door rattled open, and a woman entered. The woman searched every bit of Emily's clothing—and found nothing.

When the woman reported that there was no evidence against Emily, Rawdon let her go. He was still suspicious—but he couldn't prove she was a spy.

Emily continued on. After three days of riding, she reached the camp of General Sumter. She was hungry and tired, but happy. She stood before Sumter and recited the message she had memorized, word for word.

General Sumter assembled his troops to march toward the camp of General Greene. After the two generals joined forces near the town of Ninety Six, they attacked General Lord Rawdon's troops and, in time, they drove the British out of South Carolina.

Young people—both boys and girls, both free and slave—played important roles in the Revolution. Whether they took up a gun or went undercover as spies and messengers, the young people of the Colonies did their part for the cause of liberty.

3

Samuel Adams Started a Revolution

Samuel Adams, engraving by Charles Goodman from a painting by Copley

What is a leader? A leader is someone who inspires people to work together to achieve a goal they all want to reach. One of the most important leaders of Revolutionary times was Samuel Adams. It can truly be said that he, more than any other person, prepared the

American people for the Revolution. He inspired the people of the Thirteen Colonies to work together for the cause of freedom. But he didn't set out to be a leader. In fact, in his early years, he seemed destined to be a failure.

Samuel Adams was born in Boston, Massachusetts, in 1722, the son of a wealthy merchant. His parents sent him to the best schools, hoping he would become a Christian minister. Young Samuel worked hard at his studies and earned the second-best grades of all the students at Harvard College.

In those days the Massachusetts colony was part of the British Empire, and people were divided into separate classes—the poor *working class*, the *middle class*, and the rich and powerful *upper class*. People were expected to stay in their class, and those in the lower classes were kept out of the upper class.

The president of Harvard College was a rich, snobbish man. Because Samuel's father, a merchant, did not belong to the upper class, the college president changed Samuel's grades, moving him from second place to sixth place.

Samuel never forgot how he was forced to accept a lower grade in college simply because the college president had an unfair view of Samuel's father. He believed it was wrong to treat some people worse than others merely because their parents were from a different social class. He believed all people should be treated the same.

At Harvard, Samuel Adams studied politics. When he was twenty years old, he wrote a paper for his master's degree. The paper said that the people of Massachusetts had a right to disobey the king of England and the king's governor and officers. Samuel's professors were shocked at his revolutionary views.

Samuel Adams was ahead of his time. Thirty years later, all thirteen American colonies would rise up in rebellion against the king of England.

The Successful Failure

After graduating from college, Samuel told his father he had decided not to become a minister. His father was disappointed, but he gave Samuel a large sum of money to start his own business. It was a loan, and his father expected to be paid back. But Samuel didn't start a business. He lost half of the money on bad business deals and lent the rest to a friend who never paid him back.

Samuel Adams realized that, as a businessman, he was a failure. But he was full of ideas about how the world should be and how the government should treat people. It made him angry that the British navy would stop American ships in the middle of the ocean, kidnap American sailors, and force them to join the British navy. He believed that the high taxes Americans had to pay to King George were unfair.

In 1748, when Samuel was twenty-five years old, he started the newspaper *The Independent Advertiser*. In his newspaper, he wrote about the oppressive British government. He wrote that people have a God-given right to life, liberty, and owning property. His writings made people think, and soon, many people in Boston began to speak out against British rule.

Samuel Adams became the town tax collector in 1756. Because of his concern for people who had little money, he would let some people off without paying taxes. His kind heart made him popular with the people—but the town leaders became impatient with him. They said that if he didn't collect *all* the taxes, he would have to pay the shortage out of his own pocket. He eventually owed 8,000 British pounds—about $1.6 million in today's dollars. When he couldn't pay the taxes, the town leaders fired him.

Samuel was popular with the people, so he decided to run for political office. He was elected to the Massachusetts House of Representatives and the Boston Town Meeting. Samuel led the fight against oppressive British tax laws, such as the Sugar Act of 1764, the Stamp Act of 1765, and the Townshend Acts of 1767. He also urged the people not to buy products from Great Britain.

Riots and a Massacre

As a Christian, Samuel Adams was a peace-loving man. He didn't believe in going to war unless there was no other choice. He hoped to talk the British government into treating the people of Massachusetts fairly. At the same time, he knew that Great Britain was unlikely to behave in a peaceful way. So he worked with friends to start a secret group called the Sons of Liberty, which soon spread to all the Thirteen Colonies. The group was dedicated to opposing British tyranny.

In May 1768, when the HMS *Romney* sailed into Boston Harbor and began forcing American sailors to join the British navy, the entire city began to riot. British sailors and soldiers faced mobs of angry Boston citizens. Even the British officials who governed Boston had to gather their families and hide aboard the *Romney*.

The British government sent soldiers into Boston to stop the riots. The entire city was under a full-scale occupation by soldiers. The British soldiers marched through the streets and bossed the people around.

Finally, on March 5, 1770 (as we read in chapter 1), the city was stunned by the news that British soldiers had shot and killed five people in front of the Boston Custom House. In his newspaper, Samuel Adams gave the incident an unforgettable name: the Boston Massacre. His newspaper stories inflamed the anger of the citizens of Boston. News of the massacre spread throughout the Thirteen Colonies—and people everywhere demanded an end to British rule.

In April 1770, the British government tried to ease tensions with the colonies by ending some of the taxes on British goods. But they continued to keep a tax on tea. Samuel Adams wrote newspaper stories urging people to stop buying *all* British goods, not just tea. He wanted to make Great Britain lose money on *all* their products sold to America until they agreed to end the tea tax. He said that Great Britain was wrong to tax Americans because Americans had no representatives in the British government.

Soon the slogan spread throughout the colonies, "No taxation without representation!"

The Boston Tea Party

In late November 1773, the *Dartmouth*, a British cargo ship laden with tea, docked in Boston Harbor. Samuel Adams met with the secret group the Sons of Liberty. Then he called an emergency town meeting, and several thousand Bostonians showed up. The people voted to demand that the *Dartmouth* leave Boston with all its tea still aboard—and that no tax would be paid. The people chose twenty-five men to stand guard and keep the ship from unloading its tea.

Two more British tea ships, the *Eleanor* and the *Beaver*, arrived in Boston Harbor. The situation was becoming a crisis, and the people were furious. On December 16, Samuel Adams called another town meeting, and about a third of the town showed up, even more than last time. There were so many people that Boston's Old South Meeting House couldn't hold them all. Hundreds stood in the streets in a bitterly cold rain, straining to hear the meeting.

Near the end of the meeting, a group of men left the Meeting House. Samuel Adams didn't take part in what happened next, though he helped plan it.

At about six that evening, a group of men approached the wharf disguised as Mohawk people so that British officials couldn't identify them. No one knows how many took part in the incident, but it may have been more than a hundred men. They boarded the *Dartmouth*, the *Eleanor*, and the *Beaver*—an event known as the Boston Tea Party.

For three hours, the men opened one chest of tea after another and dumped them into Boston Harbor. They opened more than three hundred chests in all. The men of the Boston Tea Party were careful to not damage the ships or destroy any property except the tea. They did not want to be accused of rioting or violence.

By around nine, the Sons of Liberty had finished their work. They quietly disappeared into the night.

The British government responded by imposing the Coercive Acts of 1774, a set of laws so harsh that the British thought the colonists would have to give up. But the Coercive Acts only made the colonists angrier.

Through his newspaper columns and speeches, Samuel Adams became an important leader of the American resistance to British rule. He also served in the Massachusetts Provincial Congress, an organization the British government had outlawed. The Provincial Congress formed groups of volunteer soldiers called Minutemen—fighters who were ready for battle at a minute's notice.

British officials decided to teach Samuel Adams a lesson. In April 1775, Adams learned that the British wanted to arrest him. He met with his friend John Hancock (another leader of the rebellion), and they escaped from Boston and hid in Lexington, ten miles northwest of Boston.

That decision would lead to world-changing events, including a famous midnight ride and a "shot heard 'round the world."

4

Sarah Fulton:
Mother of the Boston Tea Party

The Destruction of Tea at Boston Harbor, lithograph by Sarony & Major, 1846

orn in 1740, Sarah Bradlee Fulton was a leader of the Daughters of Liberty, a group of women from the Thirteen Colonies who supported the Revolution. Sarah lived in Medford, five miles north of Boston, and she urged people to stop buying goods from Great Britain. She hoped that, by making Britain lose money, the American people could force Britain to stop its oppression.

Some of the men who took part in the Boston Tea Party met at the home of Sarah's brother, Nathaniel Bradlee. It was Sarah's idea to disguise the men as Mohawk people so British officials wouldn't recognize them. In the kitchen of her brother's home, Sarah helped paint the faces of the men.

On December 16, 1773, at a little before six that evening, the men of the Boston Tea Party headed for the wharf where three British ships were anchored. The men boarded the ships, opened the chests, and dumped the tea into the harbor.

Because of the role she played in planning this act of protest, Sarah Bradlee Fulton became known as the "Mother of the Boston Tea Party."

But this was not the only part she played in the Revolutionary War.

A Leader of Nurses

On June 17, 1775, the British and American armies fought on the hills overlooking Boston Harbor. This fierce and dramatic battle (which we'll explore in exciting detail in chapters 10 and 11) became known as the Battle of Bunker Hill.

At sunset after the battle, the American militiamen brought their wounded fighters into Medford. Sarah quickly organized the women of the town into a team of nurses, and they set up a makeshift hospital on the lawn in front of a tavern. Sarah acted as a leader, calmly directing the other women caring for the wounded fighters.

One of the wounded soldiers had a bullet injury in his face. Sarah removed the bullet and sewed up the wound with thread. She soon forgot that she had helped this man, because there were so many soldiers to care for. But years later, the man visited Sarah, showed her the scar where he'd been shot, and thanked her for removing the bullet.

"Shoot Away!"

Early in the war, the British surrounded the city of Boston. British army patrols roamed the countryside, bullying farmers and townspeople. One time, a group of Patriots hauled a load of wood by oxcart, trying to get the wood to the troops at Cambridge. The soldiers needed this wood in order to keep warm and cook their food. The oxcart was supposed to come through Medford—but word reached Sarah Bradlee Fulton that British soldiers waited on the road to take the wood for themselves.

Sarah sent her husband out to meet the shipment, buy the wood, and bring it to their Medford home. They would keep the wood hidden until it was safe to move it to Cambridge. Her husband went out—and ran into a squad of British soldiers who had already captured the oxcart. He returned home empty-handed and told Sarah that the Redcoats had stolen the load.

Furious, Sarah put on a shawl and went out on foot. She found the troops on the road and dashed out in front of their oxen. She grasped the two oxen by the horns and began turning them in the opposite direction.

"Let go of those oxen," a soldier said, "or we'll shoot you!"

Sarah shouted, "Shoot away!"

She continued turning the oxen around.

The British troops took aim at Sarah—then they lowered their muskets. She had won. The soldiers allowed Sarah to take the oxen and the cartload of wood.

General Washington's Messenger

Another time, Sarah volunteered to take a message to a spy behind enemy lines in Boston. She walked four miles by night to the waterfront village of Charlestown. Finding a rowboat tied to the dock, she got in and rowed across the Charles River. She reached the home of the spy and delivered the message.

She returned home, arriving at her doorstep as the sun was rising. She had walked all night, and she was tired but happy that she had completed her mission.

A few days later, she opened her door—and there stood General George Washington himself. He had come to Medford to personally thank Sarah for her courageous service. Sarah served a fruit punch to General Washington from her new punch bowl with its silver ladle. She would always remember that moment as the proudest moment of her life—and the chair the general sat in would forever be known as the "General Washington Chair."

5

John Hancock Risked His Fortune for Freedom

John Hancock by John Singleton Copley

I n April 1775, Samuel Adams and his friend John Hancock had left Boston to hide from the British in the village of Lexington, Massachusetts. On the night of April 18, General Thomas Gage, commander of the British forces in North America, sent soldiers to Lexington and Concord with orders to capture Adams and Hancock. Who was Samuel Adams's friend John Hancock—and why were the British so desperate to capture him?

John Hancock: A Wanted Man

Born in January 1737, John Hancock was raised by his uncle Thomas Hancock, a wealthy Boston merchant. John graduated from Harvard College in 1754 and went to work for his uncle Thomas. He later inherited his uncle's business and became one of the wealthiest men in the Thirteen Colonies.

John Hancock was famous for giving money to widows and the poor. He saw how the heavy taxes of Great Britain made it hard for people to make a living. He soon began using his wealth to buy tents, horses, guns, and ammunition for American militias.

In 1765, John Hancock was elected as a Boston town official. It was a time of rising Patriot anger against British rule. In June 1768, British customs officials took control of a ship Hancock owned, a sloop called the *Liberty*. Without evidence, British officials accused Hancock of smuggling—illegally transporting goods into America without paying taxes. A judge later dismissed the charge for lack of evidence.

The British mistreatment of John Hancock enraged the people of Boston and led to rioting. The British sent troops to Boston to occupy the city and bully the people into obedience.

After the Boston Massacre in March 1770, John Hancock and Samuel Adams met with the British governor of Massachusetts, Thomas Hutchinson. They convinced the governor that the only way to bring calm to the city was to move the

British soldiers to Castle William, a British fort on an island in Boston Harbor. Because he persuaded the governor to remove the soldiers, Hancock became more popular than ever in Boston—and more hated than ever by the British.

In December 1774, Massachusetts sent John Hancock as a delegate to the Second Continental Congress. The Congress was a gathering of representatives of all the Thirteen Colonies. In May 1775, the representatives elected Hancock president of the Second Continental Congress.

Because of Hancock's growing popularity and political influence, the British began to fear him. They declared him and Samuel Adams to be wanted men. In June 1775, British General Thomas Gage declared John Hancock and Samuel Adams to be enemies of Great Britain.

This announcement was a big mistake for Great Britain. It made Hancock and Adams instantly famous and turned them into heroes. The following year, on August 2, 1776, John Hancock—as the president of the Second Continental Congress—would write the first, largest, and boldest signature on the Declaration of Independence.

It was Hancock's way of declaring his own defiance toward Great Britain and King George III.

6

Paul Revere: Midnight Rider

Paul Revere Arousing Hancock and Adams by Henry Hintermeister

On the evening of April 18, 1775, Samuel Adams and John Hancock were in Lexington, Massachusetts, resting at the home of Jonas Clarke, pastor of the Church of Christ. Pastor Clarke had offered them a safe refuge from the British soldiers who were searching for them.

At the same time in Boston, a Patriot leader, Dr. Joseph Warren, handed a message to a Patriot named Paul Revere. The message said British troops were crossing the Charles River in Boston and heading toward Lexington, ten miles away. In moments, Paul Revere would begin his famous "midnight ride" to warn colonial militias that British soldiers were coming.

Who was Paul Revere? What role did his midnight ride play in the American Revolution?

The Christian Secret Agent

Paul Revere was born on New Year's Day, 1735. By profession, he was a silversmith and engraver. He had learned the metalworking trade from his French-born father, Apollos Rivoire, who later changed his last name to Revere. Paul Revere was a Christian who never missed a Sunday service at Boston's New Brick Church.

In his early career, Revere was a prosperous businessman, but his business suffered when Great Britain imposed the Stamp Act of 1765. The taxes of the Stamp Act hurt businesses so badly that many business owners went bankrupt. Revere had to go into debt to keep his business running.

Paul Revere learned dentistry from a surgeon, and he made extra money carving false teeth and dentures. One of his dental clients was Dr. Joseph Warren. Revere and Dr. Warren both joined the Sons of Liberty, founded by Samuel Adams. Members of this group used secret passwords to prove they were indeed members.

When the tea-laden merchant ship *Dartmouth* docked in Boston Harbor, Revere and Dr. Warren were two of the citizens who stood guard at the wharf so the ship could not be unloaded. They probably took part in the Boston Tea Party as well.

Today, the United States Central Intelligence Agency (or CIA) names Paul Revere as one of America's first and most important secret agents. In addition to being a member of the Sons of Liberty, he served with a Boston spy network called the Mechanics. Revere and his fellow Mechanics would gather information and send warnings of British troop movements.

The thirty members of the Mechanics held regular meetings at the Green Dragon Tavern in Boston's North End. They kept watch on the activities of British soldiers and the movement of British weapons and supplies. The information they gathered led Dr. Warren to warn Revere that the British were heading for the village of Lexington, looking for Samuel Adams and John Hancock.

The Midnight Rider

During the evening of April 18, 1775, Dr. Warren gave Paul Revere the assignment of riding to Lexington and warning the Minutemen along the way that British troops were on the march. Dr. Warren told Revere that Samuel Adams and John Hancock were staying with Pastor Jonas Clarke in Lexington.

Paul Revere arranged for a friend to hang either one or two lanterns in the steeple of the Old North Church. In case Revere was stopped by the British, the lanterns would serve as a backup signal so that other riders could spread the news of the British troop movements. The signal was given to Revere in these memorable words: "One if by land, two if by sea." One lantern meant that the British troops would take the land route through Boston Neck. Two lanterns would mean that the troops would take boats across the Charles River.

After putting on an overcoat and boots, Revere went to the waterfront. Friends rowed him in a boat through the darkness. Arriving at Charlestown, he met with members of the Sons of Liberty. One of them lent him a horse named Brown Beauty, and Revere set off on his mission. It was about eleven o'clock.

He rode through Medford and gave the message to the captain of the Medford militia. Then he rode on toward Lexington, stopping at houses along the way, warning the militiamen that the British army would be coming up the road from Boston. Revere was careful to ride in silence, hoping not to be noticed by any British patrols.

He reached the Lexington home of Pastor Jonas Clarke sometime after midnight and shouted to a militiaman who stood guard by the house. The militiaman told him to stop making noise. Revere replied that there was about to be a lot of noise because the British army was coming.

Inside the house, John Hancock heard Paul Revere's arrival. He opened the door and invited the midnight rider in. As Revere was having food and drink, getting ready to ride on to nearby Concord, his friend William Dawes arrived. Dawes had seen the lanterns in the church steeple and had also spread the word.

Paul Revere and William Dawes got on their horses and set off together for Concord. They were soon joined by another Patriot, Dr. Samuel Prescott. The three rode together for a while—then they were stopped by a squad of British soldiers.

Prescott and Dawes managed to escape, riding hard as the soldiers fired their muskets at them. But Revere's path was blocked. The soldiers forced him into a pasture. They ordered him down from his horse and threatened to shoot him. Then they questioned him and took his horse away.

Without a horse to ride, Revere walked back toward Lexington.

As he reached the outskirts of the village in the early morning of April 19, 1775, he worried about the British troops. And he had good reason to worry. In the middle of town on Lexington Green, the first battle of the Revolutionary War would soon begin.

7

Jonas Clarke: Revolutionary Preacher

Photo of Lexington Green in 2009 by John Phelan. Pastor Jonas Clarke's original church building is no longer standing. The church in the center of the picture was built in 1847. The Soldier's Monument on the left was placed on the Green in 1799.

For years, Pastor Jonas Clarke had seen his people suffering under the brutal oppression of King George and the British army. Week by week, he had been preparing his people for battle. Sunday after Sunday, he had preached sermons about courage and faith in the face of tyranny.

The night of April 18, his houseguests Samuel Adams and John Hancock had asked him if the people would fight when the British army came.

"I have trained them for this very hour," Pastor Clarke told them. "They would fight and, if need be, die, too, under the shadow of the house of God."

Now the hour had come. On the morning of April 19, 1775, the sun was rising over Lexington Green, the triangle-shaped grassy area in the middle of town.

A messenger brought the news to Pastor Clarke that the British soldiers were approaching on the road from the southeast. Pastor Clarke ran to the church and rang the bell, calling the Lexington militiamen to assemble on the Green. The militia drummer went out on the street, beating a rhythm on his snare drum.

Forty men of the Lexington Militia ran onto the north end of the Green. Another thirty militiamen took hidden positions next to the buildings that surrounded the area. Captain John Parker, a deacon of the church, lined up his men in battle formation and ordered them to load their muskets. Women, children, and men who were too old to fight gathered in small groups across from the Green to watch the battle.

The Arrival of the Redcoats

From the southeast came the sound of drums and tramping boots. Four hundred British Redcoats, commanded by Major John Pitcairn, marched into town double-quick. Pitcairn, on horseback, assembled his troops into two ranks at the south end of Lexington Green. Then he rode in front of his troops and demanded that the Lexington militiamen throw down their muskets.

The Americans were badly outnumbered. There were six well-trained British soldiers for every American militiaman. Captain Parker knew his men didn't have a fighting chance. He ordered his men to walk away from the Green but to keep their muskets in hand.

As the militiamen walked away, someone fired a gun. To this day, no one knows if the gun was fired on purpose or by accident—or whether it was a British or American gun.

But that first gunshot became known as "the shot heard 'round the world"—the opening shot of the Revolutionary War.

The Redcoats opened fire on the Americans, just forty yards away. Pitcairn shouted at his soldiers to stop shooting, but he was unable to control his men.

The militiamen scattered. Some turned and fired at the Redcoats.

When the British had spent their ammunition, they made a bayonet charge and drove the militiamen off the Green. Just then, another British officer, Lieutenant Colonel Frances Smith, arrived with more troops. Together, Pitcairn and Smith shouted orders and tried to get their troops to stop shooting.

The Sorrow of Pastor Clarke

Paul Revere arrived moments after the battle ended. He saw the bodies of the dead and dying on the Green. He watched helplessly as the British soldiers lined up in two columns and fired a round of victory shots in the air. They shouted three times, then started marching, headed toward the village of Concord.

In the battle on Lexington Green, eight American militiamen died. One British soldier suffered a minor wound. The Americans had lost the first battle of the American Revolution—but their bravery and dedication changed history.

After the battle, Pastor Jonas Clarke tended to the wounded and dying. His heart was broken over the men who had spilled their blood on Lexington Green. But Pastor Clarke had great hope for the future. His eyes welling with tears, he said, "From this day will be dated the liberty of the world."

8

Samuel Whittemore:
Oldest Soldier of the Revolution

The Minute Men, statue by Daniel Chester French at the
Old North Bridge, Concord, Massachusetts

The British troops marched from Lexington to Concord,
where they searched homes, shops, and farms for hidden weapons. At Concord's North Bridge at eleven in
the morning, a force of four hundred American militiamen

surprised one hundred of the king's troops. The outnumbered Redcoats retreated and joined up with other British troops in Concord.

Then the British soldiers started back the way they came. As the Redcoats marched toward Boston, American militiamen shot at them from behind trees and stone fences.

One of the Americans who attacked the retreating British troops was a seventy-eight-year-old veteran named Samuel Whittemore—the oldest soldier of the Revolutionary War. Thirty years earlier, Whittemore had fought against the French in Nova Scotia and had captured a sword from a French officer. In another battle, Whittemore had won a pair of dueling pistols.

On the day of the Battles of Lexington and Concord, Samuel Whittemore was farming in his field when he saw a brigade of British Grenadiers moving down the road. Whittemore positioned himself behind a stone wall, loaded his single-shot musket, and fired, killing one soldier. Then he drew his dueling pistols and shot two more British soldiers.

The Grenadiers spotted Whittemore and saw that he was out of ammunition. As they crossed the field toward him, he drew his sword and ran straight at the British soldiers. One of the Grenadiers fired, shooting Whittemore in the face. He fell to the ground and the other Grenadiers surrounded him, attacking him with their bayonets and musket butts. They left him bleeding on the ground.

Minutes later, a group of American militiamen came down the road, looking for Redcoats. They saw Samuel Whittemore on his knees in his field, attempting to load his musket. He was getting ready to hunt down the British Grenadiers who had wounded him. The militiamen had to hold him down and talk him into seeing a doctor.

That night, the doctor in Medford treated Whittemore's wounds. The doctor told the man's friends that Whittemore would probably die before morning.

But Samuel Whittemore didn't die. He recovered from his wounds and saw America become a free nation. He lived eighteen more years, till the age of ninety-six. Samuel Whittemore was an example of courage, patriotism, and perseverance to the end of his days.

9

Governor Trumbull's Day of Prayer

Jonathan Trumbull, engraving 1885 by
E. Mackenzie after a painting by Col. John
Trumbull

A month before the Battles of Lexington and Concord, Jonathan Trumbull Sr., the governor of the colony of Connecticut, asked his people to join him in a day of prayer. He didn't know that the date he chose for this day of prayer—April 19, 1775—would be the day of the opening battles of the American Revolution.

In his proclamation, Governor Trumbull asked the people to pray that God would "restore, preserve, and secure the Liberties of this and all the other British American colonies, and make the Land a mountain of Holiness and Habitation of Righteousness forever." At the same time as the people of Connecticut were praying for liberty and righteousness, war erupted in Massachusetts.

King George III had first appointed Trumbull deputy governor of the Connecticut colony in 1766. After Governor William Pitkin died in 1769, Trumbull became governor. Governor Trumbull became increasingly troubled by Britain's oppression of the American colonists. Though Governor Trumbull had hoped for a peaceful relationship with the "mother country," he could see that the American colonies were headed for war with Great Britain.

In May 1774, General Thomas Gage became the British military governor of Massachusetts. After the Battles of Lexington and Concord, General Gage sent Governor Trumbull a letter asking for Trumbull's help in stopping the riots in Massachusetts.

Governor Trumbull wrote back, saying that his sympathies were with the American Patriots, not King George. He scolded Gage for the British occupation of Boston and for the "most unprovoked attack" against the citizens of Lexington and Concord. He called Gage's actions "outrages" that would "disgrace even barbarians."

Though Governor Trumbull had been appointed by King George, his conscience belonged to God and to the people of Connecticut—not to the king of England.

When King George heard that Governor Trumbull sided with the American cause, he wanted to remove Trumbull from office—but he couldn't. The outbreak of war between Great Britain and the Thirteen Colonies meant that the king no longer controlled Connecticut. Trumbull had won the admiration of the people and had become a leader in the Revolution.

Governor Trumbull was a trusted friend to General George Washington throughout the Revolutionary War. Trumbull was in charge of paying the soldiers of the Continental army. Washington knew he could always turn to "Brother Jonathan" in a time of need.

At the end of the war, the Continental army offered Trumbull money for his service in the war. He wouldn't take the money for himself. Instead, he gave it to needy soldiers.

Jonathan Trumbull Sr. was a man of conscience and a man of prayer. Though he had been appointed by the tyrant King George III, God chose him to help lead the Americans to freedom.

10

Henry Knox: Bookstore Clerk Who Became a General

Hauling Guns by Ox Teams from Fort Ticonderoga for the Siege of Boston, artist unknown

Henry Knox was born in 1750. His father, a ship's captain, died when Henry was nine years old. Henry's mother had no money, so Knox left school to get a job and support his family. He worked as a clerk in a Boston bookstore. The shop owner was kind to him and let him borrow books to read at home. Knox learned many subjects from books, including French and mathematics.

In March 1770, Knox stood in the snow outside the Boston Custom House. He saw the crowd shouting and throwing snowballs at the British soldiers—and he knew the situation was dangerous. He begged the soldiers to lower their weapons and leave before someone got hurt. He was a witness as the soldiers fired their weapons and killed five Boston citizens. The memory of the Boston Massacre left a deep mark on his soul.

Knox opened his own bookstore in 1771, when he was twenty-one. He often took home books on history and military science. He had a special interest in the science of artillery—how to use mathematics to calculate the distance, angle, and weight of the cannonball, and the explosive force needed to hit a distant target.

He was a member of the Sons of Liberty, and historians believe he took part in the Boston Tea Party. When the Revolutionary War broke out in Lexington and Concord, Henry and his wife Lucy closed the bookstore and escaped from British-occupied Boston.

While he and Lucy were escaping the city, American militia groups moved into the hills around Boston. The militias blocked the roads leading out of Boston and kept the British army trapped in the city.

Henry Knox joined a militia and told the commander, General Artemas Ward, that he had studied artillery science from books. General Ward knew that none of his militiamen knew how to aim cannons with any accuracy. So he had

Henry Knox train some of the militia volunteers to become expert artillerymen.

Tested at the Battle of Bunker Hill

On June 12, 1775, General Thomas Gage, commander of British forces, demanded that the American rebels in nearby Charlestown surrender. The rebels refused General Gage's demand. They knew that Gage was planning an attack.

The American commanders decided to take control of two high places outside of Charlestown—Bunker Hill and Breed's Hill. On June 16, Henry Knox led 1,200 militiamen up Breed's Hill. There they built a line of fortifications, including cannons.

The next afternoon, Knox looked out from the unfinished fortification and saw twenty-eight British barges crossing the river and heading toward Charlestown. The British were attacking with three thousand troops.

Knox had his men bring up the cannons. His men figured out the distance, the angle, and the explosive charge. Then they fired at the British, just as Knox had taught them.

Meanwhile, four British battleships that were anchored on the Charles River saw the smoke from the cannons atop Breed's Hill. They aimed their cannons at Breed's Hill and sent a barrage of cannonballs raining all around Henry Knox and his men. In spite of the British cannon fire, the Americans refused to retreat. They continued firing their cannons, slowing the British troops who came ashore from the barges.

The British ran through the town of Charlestown with flaming torches and set the wooden buildings on fire. Soon, the whole town of Charlestown was aflame. The British then divided their force and approached Breed's Hill from two sides.

For the Americans atop the hill, the uniforms of the Redcoats made a bright target against the green grass. American militiamen fired their muskets, and Knox's artillerymen blasted cannon fire through the British troops. The Redcoats fell dead or wounded by the dozens. Terrified British soldiers retreated, scrambling for safety from the American muskets and cannons.

After a few minutes' rest, the British launched a second charge up the hill. Again, they were forced back by the roar of cannons and the crack of musket fire. However, the British commanders could tell that the American attack was weaker this time. The Americans were running out of gunpowder.

The Redcoats fixed bayonets onto their muskets and charged up Breed's Hill again. The Americans had no bayonets and were out of gunpowder. They were nearly defenseless—yet they refused to retreat. The Americans met the British at the hilltop and the two armies fought with lunging blades, musket butts, clubs, fists, and chokeholds.

The British were astonished at how fiercely the Americans fought, even though they were out of ammunition. Finally, the American commander saw that his soldiers were so badly outnumbered that it would be useless to remain. He called for his men to retreat. As the Americans ran down Breed's Hill, the British were too exhausted to chase them.

Though the battle took place mostly on Breed's Hill, it became known as the Battle of Bunker Hill (no one is sure why). The Americans suffered 115 dead, 305 wounded, and 30 captured. The British suffered 226 dead (including 19 officers) and 828 wounded (including 62 officers) for a total of 1,054 casualties. The British had won the battle but had paid a much higher price than the Americans.

The day after the battle, the British commander General William Howe wrote in a letter to his brother, a naval admiral, "The success is too dearly bought."

The battle would have ended in total disaster for the Americans if not for Henry Knox and his expert use of artillery. General Howe never regained his confidence as a military leader after that battle.

Who was Henry Knox? Before the Revolutionary War, he was just a bookseller from Boston who had read a lot about cannons. After the battle on Breed's Hill, Knox became one of the most important military leaders in the Revolutionary War.

Knox's "Noble Train of Artillery"

On July 2, 1775, General George Washington arrived at the American militia camp near Boston. The Second Continental Congress had appointed him commander in chief of the Continental army three weeks earlier. Washington was impressed by Knox's use of artillery. The forty-three-year-old Washington and the twenty-five-year-old Knox quickly became friends—and their friendship would continue long after the war.

Henry Knox heard that an American force had captured two forts in the colony of New York—Fort Ticonderoga and Fort Crown Point. He proposed a plan to General Washington. What if Knox could take some men to those forts in New York and bring their cannons back to Boston? Knox believed that, with the extra cannons, the Americans could force the British to leave Boston.

It was a daring plan. Knox would have to haul the captured cannons on wooden sleds across Massachusetts, through three hundred miles of backwoods trails, dense forests, and dangerous swamps. He would have to take the heavy cannons over two frozen rivers, hoping the ice wouldn't break.

General Washington approved Knox's plan and gave him a thousand British pounds—worth about $250,000 today—to pay for his journey. The general was taking a big risk, trusting the twenty-five-year-old bookseller with such a vital and costly mission.

On November 17, 1775, Henry Knox and his troops left Washington's camp. They arrived at Fort Ticonderoga on December 5. There, Knox and his troops took possession of a twenty-four-pounder (a gun that fired a twenty-four-pound cannonball), thirteen eighteen-pounder cannons, and ten twelve-pounder cannons, plus two howitzers, fourteen mortars, and assorted smaller guns.

Henry Knox and his men moved the heavy guns by boat and by horse and sled to Lake George. They loaded the guns on three boats and set out across the lake. One of the boats sank in shallow water, but they refloated it and got all the guns safely across the lake. As they reached the shore, snow began to fall. Knox was happy. Snow would make it easier to pull the guns by sled.

Knox called his gun caravan a "Noble train of Artillery." His journey took more than forty days. The river crossings were more difficult than Knox expected because several cannons broke through the ice. Each time, Knox's troops pulled the heavy guns from the freezing water.

On January 27, 1776, Henry Knox led his weary team into General Washington's camp. Their horses and oxen pulled sleds loaded with cannons.

In March, General Washington captured Dorchester Heights, overlooking Boston Harbor. Henry Knox placed cannons around the Heights. When General William Howe looked up and saw that the Americans could rain cannon fire on his army all across Boston, he hastily ordered his troops onto the ships. The British retreated to Halifax, Nova Scotia, more than four hundred miles away.

The British occupation of Boston was over.

Always at Washington's Side

Henry Knox was at General Washington's side on Christmas night, 1776, when Washington and his troops crossed the Delaware River to capture Trenton, New Jersey. On Knox's orders, the American troops loaded soldiers, horses, and eighteen pieces of artillery onto boats. Not a single man or gun was lost during the crossing. As a result of Knox's leadership, Washington's forces caught the enemy by surprise. Trenton was easily captured.

Henry Knox also placed the cannons at Yorktown, Virginia, that enabled the Americans to win the Revolutionary War on October 19, 1781. Afterward, he was promoted to major general. He stood at General Washington's side as the commander in chief delivered his farewell address to his officers in New York City on December 4, 1783. Knox later served as the secretary of war when Washington became the first president of the United States.

These are impressive accomplishments for a man who learned the science of warfare by reading books.

11

Peter Salem: Black Hero of Bunker Hill

Peter Salem by Walter J. Williams, Jr.

Peter Salem was born into slavery in Framingham, Massachusetts, on October 1, 1750. When he was twenty-five years old, the slave master sold him to a man named Lawson Buckminster, a major in the Continental army. Young Peter wanted to serve in the Patriot militia as a Minuteman and fight against the British, but it was against regulations for slaves to serve in the militias. Buckminster set Peter free so he could enlist.

Peter fought in the first two battles of the Revolutionary War—the Battles of Lexington and Concord—and many others. Throughout the Revolution, he fought alongside other Black militiamen, including Salem Poor, Titus Coburn, and Seymour Burr.

On June 17, 1775, Peter Salem was one of the soldiers who helped build the fortifications atop Breed's Hill, where Henry Knox was placing his cannons. Peter led a squad of men who built a defensive barrier on the hill. From behind that barrier, Peter and his squad fought hard as the British charged up the hill.

The Americans forced the British to retreat after their first charge. The Redcoats regrouped and made a second charge up the hill.

Facing the Redcoats at Close Range

Peter and his fellow militiamen had only thirteen bullets each. To make sure that each shot counted, they waited until the British soldiers were just a few yards away—then they rose up and fired. They rarely missed at such close range.

When Peter Salem stood, he faced a Redcoat in an officer's uniform, decorated with gold braid. The British officer waved his sword and shouted at the American rebels to surrender. Peter Salem aimed his musket at the officer's chest and fired a fatal shot. The officer fell backward and died instantly. That British officer was Major John Pitcairn, who had served in the occupation of Boston and commanded British forces against the Americans at Lexington and Concord.

The death of Major Pitcairn dealt a huge blow to the morale of the British army and a significant boost of confidence for the Patriots. The militiamen fought with new strength and courage, forcing the British to retreat. It wasn't until the Americans were completely out of ammunition that they finally retreated from Breed's Hill.

Peter Salem continued to serve in the Patriot army, fighting bravely at the Battle of Harlem Heights, the two Battles of Saratoga, and the Battle of Stony Point in New York, as well as the Battle of Trenton and the Battle of Monmouth Court House in New Jersey. He served in the American army until 1780, when he retired after earning a place of honor in Revolutionary War history.

12

Benjamin Franklin: The First American

Benjamin Franklin by Joseph Siffrein Duplessis

On July 4, 1776, the Second Continental Congress formally approved the Declaration of Independence. In soaring language, the Declaration made an impassioned case for human liberty and individual rights.

The Declaration of Independence was a statement of bold, courageous defiance. If the American Revolution failed, the leaders of the Revolution—including every signer of the Declaration—would be tried and executed as a traitor.

By the time the Declaration of Independence was announced, the Revolutionary War had been raging for sixteen months—and it was going badly for the Americans. The British were on the verge of capturing New York City. Many colonists were beginning to doubt that Great Britain could be beaten.

On that very first Independence Day, July 4, 1776, John Hancock of Massachusetts spoke, stressing the need for unity among the delegates. "We must be unanimous," he said. "We must all hang together."

Pennsylvania delegate Benjamin Franklin replied, "We must indeed all hang together—or, most assuredly, we shall all hang separately." Ben Franklin earned the title the "First American" because of his passion for a free and unified America.

Ben's Difficult Early Years

Benjamin Franklin was one of the most amazing and brilliant people who ever lived. He was a writer, a printer, a scientist, an inventor, a musician, a statesman, and the organizer of the nation's first post office, fire department, and public library.

Born in Boston in 1706, young Ben grew up working in his father's shop as he helped make candles and soap. Though he disliked candlemaking and soap-boiling, Ben worked hard and used the money he earned to buy books.

When he wasn't working or reading, he would go to the river to swim, row, or sail. His friends looked up to him as a leader.

When Ben was a teenager, he worked for his older brother James, who owned a print shop in Boston. James didn't pay Ben for working, other than a small allowance for meals. James expected Ben to work for free while learning the printing trade. Ben would eat the cheapest food he could buy—usually a biscuit and a few raisins—so he could save money to buy more books.

Benjamin's brother James was often cruel. If he didn't think Ben was working hard enough, or if they got into an argument, James would sometimes beat Ben. When Ben was seventeen, he angrily walked out of the print shop, never to return. He sold some of his books and used the money to pay for a boat ticket to New York. When he couldn't find a job there, he took a sailboat to New Jersey. He walked fifty miles in a rainstorm across New Jersey, then took a boat up the Delaware River to Philadelphia.

He got a job at a print shop in Philadelphia. The governor of the Pennsylvania colony said he would give Ben a loan to start his own print shop.

Ben sailed to England to buy a printing press for his business, and the governor was supposed to send the money to London—but the governor didn't keep his promise. At eighteen, Ben was stranded in London without money or friends. He spent two years working and saving up money to return to America.

In 1726, Ben returned to Philadelphia, borrowed money, and opened a print shop of his own.

A Plan for Moral Perfection

In his early twenties, Benjamin Franklin wrote down his "Plan for Attaining Moral Perfection." He listed thirteen virtues to practice every day. They were:

1. Temperance (don't eat too much or get drunk)
2. Silence (say only what is helpful to others and yourself)
3. Order (live a neat, clean, and disciplined life)
4. Resolution (do the things that are most important, even when they are hard)
5. Frugality (don't waste money)
6. Industry (work hard, and don't waste time)
7. Sincerity (be honest and do right—never lie)
8. Justice (do your duty to others, and don't hurt anyone)
9. Moderation (avoid extremes)
10. Cleanliness (keep your body, clothing, and home clean and tidy)
11. Tranquility (be calm, and don't let problems upset you)
12. Chastity (live a modest and pure life)
13. Humility (don't think too highly of yourself—imitate Jesus and Socrates)

Benjamin Franklin published wise observations in a series of books he called *Poor Richard's Almanack*. He began the series when he was twenty-six, and he published a new edition every year from 1733 to 1758. Some of his sayings are still famous today:

"Early to bed and early to rise makes a man healthy, wealthy, and wise."

"There are no gains without pains."

"He that cannot obey cannot command."

"Haste makes waste."

He was a self-educated man, thanks to the many books he read. He loved science, and he founded an academy that became the University of Pennsylvania.

Ben believed that lightning was a form of electricity. He set out to prove it by flying a silk kite outside during a thunderstorm. An iron key dangled from the kite. After the kite had been in the sky for a while, he brought it down and placed his hand near the key. Bright sparks of electricity jumped from the key to his hand.

When he published his findings, he became world-

Title page for *Poor Richard*, 1743, an almanack printed by Benjamin Franklin

famous. Several European universities gave him an honorary doctorate degree.

Man of Achievement, Man of Humility

In 1754, long before the outbreak of the Revolutionary War, Benjamin Franklin proposed a "Plan of Union" for the Thirteen Colonies. He wanted to unite the colonies to fight against foreign enemies. The plan failed, but it forced many American leaders to think about the need for unity in the struggle against British tyranny.

In June 1776, Ben was chosen to serve on a "Committee of Five" to write the Declaration of Independence. The other members of the committee were John Adams (a cousin of Samuel Adams), Thomas Jefferson, Robert Livingston, and Roger Sherman. After the Declaration of Independence was approved on July 4, 1776, the Second Continental Congress sent Ben to France to ask for money to aid the fight against Great Britain.

The people of France welcomed Ben with parades and parties. Now seventy years old, he charmed the leaders and common people of France. The French government gave money and military support to the new American nation. Ben remained in Paris for the next ten years.

Though Benjamin Franklin was never a governor or president and had never served in the military, he was one of America's greatest statesmen. Throughout his life, he kept his focus on the goal he had set for himself. The man who patterned his life after Jesus and Socrates found greatness through humility.

13

Esther De Berdt Reed: Fundraiser for Liberty

Esther de Berdt Reed by Charles Peale

Esther De Berdt was an English woman, born in London in 1746. She loved to read books on many subjects—and one of her favorite subjects was politics and the way governments treated their people. She hated the way the government of Great Britain treated the American colonists—and she wanted to help the American cause.

In 1763, at age seventeen, Esther met Joseph Reed, an American who had come to London to study law. They fell in love but had to spend many years apart, keeping their romance alive through letters carried between England and America by ships.

When Esther's father died in 1769, Joseph came to England and helped Esther's family put their finances in order. Esther and Joseph were married on May 31, 1770. In October, the young couple, along with Esther's mother, sailed to America to settle in Philadelphia.

In a November 1774 letter to her brother in England, Esther wrote that the Americans "are prepared for the worst" and prepared to defend their liberty "with their lives."

Esther's husband Joseph was elected to the First Continental Congress in 1774. Joseph and Esther became friends with many delegates to Congress, including General George Washington of Virginia.

When Esther received word of the Battles of Lexington and Concord in Massachusetts, she wrote to her brother, "You see every person willing to sacrifice his private interest in this glorious contest. . . . It has at least a chance to be victorious. I believe it *will*."

Raising Money, Sewing Shirts

In 1775, Esther's husband Joseph joined General Washington's staff. Esther stayed home in Philadelphia, raising their six children. She had an escape plan in case British soldiers invaded Philadelphia. Several times, she gathered her children and escaped to another city. During one of

73

these journeys, her little daughter caught smallpox and died.

In 1778, in the midst of the war, her husband Joseph was elected governor of Pennsylvania, and the family was reunited in Philadelphia.

By 1780, the Revolutionary War was in its fifth year. The Continental army suffered from shortages of food, clothing, and shoes. Esther published a pamphlet called *Sentiments of an American Woman*, explaining how women could show their patriotism by raising money to support the troops. Hundreds of women took the pamphlets from door to door, first in Philadelphia, and then throughout the Thirteen Colonies.

The women raised thousands of dollars to purchase clothing for the troops. Esther organized volunteers to make shirts for soldiers. She had them sew their names into the shirts as a show of support. The women made more than 2,200 shirts for soldiers in the Continental army.

Chapters of the Ladies Association soon formed in New Jersey, Maryland, and Virginia. Esther's leadership resulted in more fundraising and more clothing for the troops.

In September 1780, Esther De Berdt Reed became sick from a disease that swept through Philadelphia. She died on September 18, 1780, one month before her thirty-fourth birthday. Her husband and her children—the oldest just ten years old—were at her side as she died. She was buried in the Arch Street Presbyterian Cemetery in Philadelphia, but her courageous spirit and her example of bold leadership live on.

14

Thomas Paine: A Pen Instead of a Gun

Thomas Paine by Élisée Reclus

Thomas Paine was an Englishman who loved America. In 1774, he was in his late thirties and working in a British government office when his boss introduced him to Benjamin Franklin. At the time, Franklin was an American diplomat. The two men had a long conversation about liberty. Franklin suggested that Thomas Paine move to America, and he gave Paine a letter of recommendation to help him find work.

Thomas Paine boarded a ship for America. Unfortunately, the ship's water barrels were filled with polluted water. Five passengers died of typhoid fever, and Paine became very sick. When his ship sailed up the Delaware River and docked in Philadelphia, Benjamin Franklin's doctor met Paine and carried him ashore on a stretcher. It took six weeks for Thomas Paine to regain his health.

In March 1775, Paine got a job as managing editor of *The Pennsylvania Journal*. One month later, war erupted in Lexington and Concord. The Revolution had begun.

The Power of *Common Sense*

In January 1776, Thomas Paine wrote a fifty-page book called *Common Sense*. Benjamin Franklin printed the first hundred copies. The book made a powerful case for American independence with such statements as this: "We have it in our power to begin the world over again. . . . The birthday of a new world is at hand, and a race of men, perhaps as numerous as all Europe contains, are to receive their portion of freedom from the event of a few months."

Common Sense was a huge bestseller, with 100,000 copies sold in just three months. By the end of the Revolutionary War, more than 500,000 copies were sold, and many people attended public readings of the book in town halls throughout the Thirteen Colonies.

Thomas Paine wrote in a passionate, popular style about the blessings of liberty. *Common Sense* made a persuasive case for America's destiny as an independent nation.

General George Washington praised both Thomas Paine and *Common Sense*. Washington viewed the book as a turning point in the cause of the Revolution. Years later, Paine would dedicate another book, *Rights of Man*, to Washington.

At the start of the Revolutionary War, about one-fifth of colonists supported the Patriot cause and another one-fifth of colonists were Loyalists who supported Great Britain. What about the vast majority, the other three-fifths? They were undecided. They didn't like British oppression and high taxes—but they weren't sure that war was the answer.

Once Britain had attacked Americans at Lexington and Concord, General Washington and the Continental Congress needed to convince more Americans to join the Revolution. Thomas Paine wrote his book at just the right time. He had a special talent for making persuasive arguments in the language of average Americans. He convinced most Americans to support and join the war.

As Revolutionary leader John Adams said, "Without the pen of the author of *Common Sense*, the sword of Washington would have been raised in vain."

Freedom Is Worth the Price

Thomas Paine took a position as assistant to General Nathanael Greene (we'll learn about the adventures of General Greene in chapter 19). During Paine's travels with the Continental army, he wrote a series of sixteen "crisis papers."

The first, *The Crisis Number I,* was published December 19, 1776. It began with these lines:

> These are the times that try men's souls. The summer soldier and the sunshine patriot will, in this crisis, shrink from the service of their country; but he that stands it now, deserves the love and thanks of man and woman. Tyranny, like hell, is not easily conquered; yet we have this consolation with us, that the harder the conflict, the more glorious the triumph. What we obtain too cheap, we esteem too lightly: it is dearness only that gives every thing its value.

Paine was telling the people that they would have to pay a price for freedom. The battle would be hard-fought and difficult—but he assured his readers that freedom was well worth the price.

The first crisis paper appeared after General Washington's army had suffered a number of defeats and setbacks. Washington was planning to make a daring and dangerous crossing of the Delaware River to Trenton, New Jersey. To boost the morale of his soldiers, Washington gave copies of Paine's crisis paper to his officers. Each officer read the paper to his troops. Paine's words inspired the Continental army to fight with a renewed sense of purpose.

Largely because of Thomas Paine's writings, the American people fought hard and reversed the tide of battle. On September 3, 1783, British rule in America came to an end. Much of the credit for America's victory belongs to Thomas Paine, who fought with a pen instead of a gun—and who inspired the American people with the dream of freedom.

15

Thomas Jefferson: The Man Who Declared Independence

Declaration of Independence by John Trumbull. The Committee of Five, in the center of the painting, are (left to right) John Adams, Roger Sherman, Robert R. Livingston, Thomas Jefferson, and Benjamin Franklin.

Thomas Jefferson was one of the most fascinating and complex people who ever lived. There's a good chance that much of what you've heard about him is either incomplete or untrue. When you've finished reading this chapter, you'll know more about the life of Thomas Jefferson than most Americans know.

Like Benjamin Franklin, Thomas Jefferson had knowledge and experience in many fields, including science, mathematics, history, politics, literature, art, architecture, and religion. In addition to English, Jefferson could read and speak five languages—Latin, Greek, French, Italian, and Spanish.

He was born April 13, 1743, the third of ten children. At age nine, he attended a boarding school. His father was a wealthy farmer and slave owner in Virginia. When Jefferson was fourteen, his father died, leaving him five thousand acres of land and a number of slaves.

In 1760, sixteen-year-old Thomas Jefferson began attending William and Mary College. One of his favorite teachers was Dr. William Small, a professor of mathematics. Dr. Small saw that Jefferson had a bright, questioning mind, and he took a special interest in his young pupil.

Dr. Small introduced Jefferson to the writings of great scientists and thinkers, such as Isaac Newton, Francis Bacon, and John Locke. Jefferson later wrote that Dr. Small's friendship "probably fixed the destinies of my life."

A Lawyer Who Defended Slaves

Jefferson completed a four-year college course in just two years, graduating in 1762. He studied law and became a lawyer in 1767. In 1768, using the knowledge of architecture he had learned from books, he began building a hilltop home he called Monticello (which means "Little Mountain" in Italian).

In 1769, Jefferson was elected to the Virginia House of Burgesses. Though he owned slaves, he wanted to reform slavery. One of his first acts as a lawmaker was to propose a law allowing slave owners to set their slaves free without getting the approval of the government. The law failed to pass.

Seven times as an attorney, Jefferson defended slaves in court. In April 1770, he defended a slave named Samuel Howell and didn't charge Howell any legal fees. Jefferson claimed that Howell should be liberated at once on the basis of natural human rights. "All men are born free," he said. "Everyone comes into the world with a right to his own person."

The judge wouldn't let Jefferson finish his argument. He ruled against Samuel Howell without listening. After the trial, Jefferson slipped some money to Howell, which the slave later used to finance his escape to freedom.

On March 27, 1775, three weeks before the outbreak of the Revolutionary War, Virginians elected Thomas Jefferson to the Second Continental Congress. At age thirty-three, he was one of the youngest members of Congress.

Self-Evident Truths

In June 1776, John Adams organized a "Committee of Five" to draft the Declaration of Independence. He selected Thomas Jefferson as one of the committee members and asked him to write the first draft.

Jefferson began writing. When he had completed a draft, he showed it to the Committee. He was horrified to watch the Committee members cutting out sentences and even whole paragraphs. Benjamin Franklin took Jefferson aside and assured him that the Committee was making the Declaration stronger and clearer by cutting out extra words.

Congress began debating the Declaration on July 1—and the members of Congress cut out even more words, including a section that criticized King George III for his support of the slave trade. Jefferson was heartbroken over these changes. He wanted the Declaration of Independence to condemn slavery. But the delegates from slaveholding states would not agree to an antislavery section of the Declaration.

The debate over the Declaration took place in a room near a horse stable. The horses attracted swarms of biting flies. Members of Congress had to debate the Declaration while swatting at the flies constantly buzzing around their heads. In fact, they were in such a hurry to get away from the flies that they approved the Declaration of Independence with very little debate.

Congress voted to accept the Declaration on July 4, 1776, and the delegates signed it on August 2. The document included one of the most famous statements on human rights ever written: "We hold these truths to be self-evident, that all men are created equal, that they are endowed by their Creator with certain unalienable Rights, that among these are Life, Liberty and the pursuit of Happiness."

Thomas Jefferson versus Benedict Arnold

Thomas Jefferson was elected governor of Virginia in 1779. One of his first acts as governor was to move Virginia's state capital from Williamsburg to Richmond. He believed

Richmond, near the center of the state, would be easier to defend than Williamsburg on the coast.

At the same time, an American general named Benedict Arnold was plotting to betray America and hand over a fort in New York in exchange for 20,000 British pounds (worth about half a million US dollars today). When General Arnold was exposed as a traitor, he escaped and joined the British army.

The British gave Benedict Arnold command of 1,600 troops in Virginia—and Arnold went on a rampage, burning towns and killing people. In January 1781, Benedict Arnold's fleet sailed up the James River to Richmond, planning to kidnap Governor Thomas Jefferson.

When Benedict Arnold's soldiers came ashore, the city of Richmond was caught by surprise. The militiamen who guarded the city fired once—then fled at the sight of hundreds of British soldiers.

When Governor Jefferson heard that Richmond was being invaded, he ordered that the militia remove the city's tobacco and military supplies—and that all the townspeople flee the city. He took his family to Tuckahoe, northwest of Richmond. By noon, Benedict Arnold's soldiers had taken control of Richmond without firing a shot.

Benedict Arnold sent a message to Governor Jefferson, demanding that Jefferson turn over the tobacco and military supplies. Jefferson sent a message back, saying he refused to bargain with a traitor.

When Benedict Arnold read Jefferson's reply, he flew into a rage. He ordered his troops to loot the town and load the stolen goods aboard the British ships. Then he ordered his men to set fire to Richmond. Strong winds sent flames exploding through the wooden buildings. Richmond burned to the ground.

News of Richmond's destruction broke Jefferson's heart—and made him angry. He sent a militia to chase the British forces. The American militia caught up with Benedict Arnold's slow-moving army and killed many British troops.

News of the burning of Richmond angered General George Washington. He offered a reward to anyone who killed or captured Benedict Arnold. Targets were printed with Benedict Arnold's face on them. Soldiers used them for target practice so they would recognize the traitor.

Six months after Richmond burned, the British made another attempt to kidnap Governor Thomas Jefferson, this time at his home in Monticello. Twenty-six-year-old Patriot Jack Jouett saw the British soldiers making camp on the road that led toward Charlottesville and Monticello.

Jouett rode forty miles to warn Jefferson that the British were coming. Jefferson and his family escaped from Monticello mere minutes before the British arrived. For his brave action, Jack Jouett is remembered as the "Paul Revere of the South."

A Slave Owner Who Opposed Slavery?

Many people wonder how Thomas Jefferson could be a slaveholder who was opposed to slavery. When he wrote the Declaration of Independence, he declared that "all men are created equal," and he tried to insert an antislavery clause. As a lawyer, he defended slaves. As a Virginia legislator, he tried to make it legal to set slaves free. Yet he continued to own slaves.

Thomas Jefferson freed two slaves during his lifetime, but he continued to own at least two hundred slaves. Under Jefferson's leadership as governor, Virginia became the first state to outlaw bringing in slaves from other states or other nations. In March 1801, Jefferson was inaugurated as the third president of the United States, and he made the international slave trade illegal throughout the United States. But he didn't abolish slavery or set the slaves in America free.

Thomas Jefferson feared what slavery was doing to America. He once wrote, "I tremble for my country when I reflect that God is just: that his justice cannot sleep forever. . . . The spirit of the master is abating, that of the slave rising from the dust."

His views were shaped by the slaveholding culture in which he lived. His father was a slave owner. Many of his friends were slave owners. Yet, in his heart, Jefferson knew that slavery was morally evil, and he often said so. Why, then, didn't he set his slaves free?

Did he think it would ruin him financially to free all of his slaves and use only hired labor to work his farm? Maybe so—but I wish he had taken that risk. I wish he had lived his life according to the principles in the Declaration of Independence. I wish Jefferson had started to abolish slavery in his own time, beginning with the slaves at Monticello.

Thomas Jefferson was a great man with a brilliant mind. He played a key role in the American Revolution. But he was also a flawed man, and he struggled with his conscience over slavery throughout his life.

We should learn the lessons from Thomas Jefferson's struggle with slavery: Make sure that your life matches what you say you believe. If you must pay a price to do the right thing, then pay the price. It may cost you everything you own, but do the right thing anyway. Treat everyone around you as a human being made in the image of God.

16

John Paul Jones: Ranger of the Sea

John Paul Jones by Charles Wilson Peale

John Paul Jr. was the son of a gardener in Scotland, born on July 6, 1747. The gardener's son grew up dreaming of adventure on the high seas.

John Paul Jr. was a natural leader as a boy. His friends would climb into rowboats and paddle out onto the water.

Then John would climb onto a rock and shout orders to the boys, pretending to be an admiral sending his fleet into battle.

He joined the British merchant marine at age thirteen, serving as a cabin boy on a slave ship. He saw how the captain and crew treated the slaves, and he hated slavery. He believed that all people had a right to be free.

At age fifteen, he left the slave ship and signed on to a cargo ship. During one voyage, a terrible disease spread through the ship, killing the captain and the first mate. Having lost their leaders, the crewmen were terrified and didn't know what to do. Though John Paul Jr. was the youngest crewman aboard, he confidently gave orders and got the ship safely into port.

As a reward, the owners placed him in command of his own ship. In 1773, his crew committed mutiny and tried to take control of the ship. John Paul Jr. acted quickly, killing the leader of the mutineers. So ended the rebellion.

Fearing that he might be tried for a crime, John Paul Jr. jumped ship and fled to Fredericksburg, Virginia, where his brother lived. He added "Jones" to his name to hide his identity and avoid arrest—and he was known as John Paul Jones for the rest of his life.

In the Continental Navy

When the Thirteen Colonies began forming the Continental navy, John Paul Jones was eager to join the Revolution. His experience earned him the rank of lieutenant, and he joined the crew of a ship called the *Alfred*.

Jones quickly demonstrated his leadership ability and was promoted to captain of the sloop *Providence*. During the summer of 1776, Jones and his crew captured sixteen British ships and raided seacoast villages in Nova Scotia. In November, Jones took command of the *Alfred* and carried out more coastal raids. He also led a rescue operation, freeing three hundred Americans who had been forced to work in British coal mines in Nova Scotia.

On June 14, 1777, he took command of the newly constructed USS *Ranger*. He set sail for France on November 1, 1777, with instructions from Congress to take command of a new frigate, the *L'Indien*, which was being built in the Netherlands.

Nearing the English coast, Jones spotted a British merchant fleet protected by the seventy-four-gun warship *Invincible*. Jones moved the *Ranger* in among the merchant ships—and the *Invincible* didn't notice that the *Ranger* was an enemy warship. Jones used the tense situation to train his crew to remain calm in the face of danger. The *Ranger* eventually slipped away unnoticed by the *Invincible*.

Arriving in France on December 2, Jones learned that the frigate Congress had promised him was no longer available. The British government had pressured the shipbuilders in the Netherlands to sell the ship to France instead. Disappointed, Jones kept the *Ranger* in port to be fitted with new masts, sails, and rigging.

While his ship was being repaired, Jones took a carriage to Paris to meet Benjamin Franklin, America's ambassador to France. Jones arrived just before Christmas. The two men became as close as father and son. Franklin introduced

Jones to many influential people and helped Jones understand how to make deals with French politicians.

Franklin also wrote new orders, instructing Captain John Paul Jones to "proceed . . . in the manner you shall judge best, for distressing the Enemies of the United States, by Sea, or otherwise, consistent with the Laws of War."

The Raids of the *Ranger*

On February 13, 1778, Jones left France aboard the newly refitted *Ranger*. In early April, the *Ranger* sank one British ship and captured another in the Irish Sea.

On April 20, the *Ranger* encountered a twenty-gun British sloop of war, the HMS *Drake*, anchored in an Irish port town. Jones wanted to sail into the harbor and attack the *Drake* in broad daylight, but his nervous crew didn't trust the daring young captain and refused to follow his orders. Jones decided to wait for another opportunity.

Next, Jones decided to raid the English port of Whitehaven. It was a daring plan. No English seaport had been raided in more than a hundred years. Jones divided his crew into two groups that went ashore at midnight on April 22.

The raid did *not* go according to the plan. One member of the landing party deserted. He ran through the town shouting that the Americans were invading. Jones and his crew disabled the town's cannons and set a fire on the waterfront but had to retreat emptyhanded. Jones got his crew back to the *Ranger* without injuries.

Though the Whitehaven raid was a failure, the news shocked the British people. Before the raid, they thought their seacoast was safe from attack. With this raid, John Paul Jones struck fear in the hearts of the English. In America, however, people were cheering. Jones quickly became famous as a daring sea captain.

On April 24, Jones spotted the HMS *Drake* leaving port and heading out to sea. The *Drake* was about the same size as the *Ranger*, and the guns of both ships were evenly matched. The British ship had an experienced captain and a well-trained crew. John Paul Jones was young and his crew sometimes disobeyed orders. But Jones was a bold and adventurous captain who was willing to take risks.

Jones followed the *Drake*, keeping the *Ranger* positioned so that the *Drake*'s captain couldn't see the *Ranger*'s guns. The British captain wondered who was following his ship. Was this mystery ship from France? Spain? Some other European country? He sent a junior lieutenant in a small boat to board the *Ranger* and find out. When the lieutenant climbed up onto the *Ranger*, Jones arrested him.

When the lieutenant didn't return, the captain of the *Drake* realized he was dealing with the famous John Paul Jones. The *Drake* raised the Union Jack, the flag of Great Britain. The *Ranger* unfurled the Stars and Stripes of the United States. The raising of flags signaled that the ships were going into battle against each other.

Jones brought the *Ranger* around in front of the *Drake* as the British were loading their cannons. Jones gave the order to fire—and the *Ranger*'s roaring cannons blasted the decks of the *Drake*.

The two ships pounded each other with cannon fire. Cannonballs shattered timbers, tore through sails and rigging, or splashed into the sea. After about an hour, Jones pointed out the *Drake*'s captain to his best marksman. Then he sent the marksman up to the fighting top—a platform near the top of the mainmast. The marksman, armed with a musket, took aim and fired—and the British captain fell dead. The battle was over. The *Drake*'s crew surrendered—and John Paul Jones took the *Drake* as his prize.

The Battle of Flamborough Head

John Paul Jones returned to France on May 8, 1778, and remained there while the *Ranger* was being repaired. He thought the *Ranger* was too small and slow, and he began looking for a larger ship with more cannons.

He bought a copy of *Les Maximes du Bonhomme Richard*, the French translation of Benjamin Franklin's *Poor Richard's Almanack*. In the book, he found a saying that would change his life: "If you want your affairs to prosper, go yourself; if not, send someone." To Jones, this meant that if he wanted a new ship, he should not send someone else to speak for him. He should go in person and ask the king of France for a ship.

John Paul Jones went to the palace at Versailles and spoke to King Louis XVI—and the king agreed to give him the *Duc de Duras*, a fourteen-year-old forty-gun warship. It was not a fast ship, as Jones had hoped for, but it had more cannons than the *Ranger*.

He took command of the *Duc de Duras* on February 4, 1779. In honor of Benjamin Franklin's advice in *Poor Richard's Almanack*, Jones renamed the ship *Bonhomme Richard*.

On August 14, 1779, Jones and the *Bonhomme Richard* led a seven-ship squadron toward Ireland. Most of the ships were French, but they sailed under the American flag. Some of the French captains were not happy being bossed by a young Scotsman. The ships sailed past Ireland and around the north coast of Scotland, then down the east coast of England. Along the way, they fought and captured some smaller English ships.

On the afternoon of September 23, the *Bonhomme Richard* was off the northeast coast of England. The crew could see the cliffs of Flamborough Head. With the *Bonhomme Richard* were three well-armed ships—the *Vengeance*, the *Alliance*, and the *Pallas*.

Jones spotted a huge convoy of forty merchant ships protected by two British warships—the HMS *Serapis* and the *Countess of Scarborough*. The *Serapis* was a brand-new forty-four-gun warship, launched six months earlier. It was one of the most dreaded warships in the British navy. Both the *Serapis* and the *Bonhomme Richard* carried crews of about 320 men.

Captain Richard Pearson of the *Serapis* spotted Jones's four ships and moved to protect the merchant vessels. Signaling with flags and guns, John Paul Jones ordered the *Vengeance*, the *Alliance*, and the *Pallas* to form a line of battle behind the *Bonhomme Richard*. But the captain of the *Alliance* ignored Jones's signals. He had a plan of his own. He used the *Alliance*'s speed and handling to swing around the larger, slower *Bonhomme Richard*, and he sailed straight toward the convoy.

The second British warship, the *Countess of Scarborough*, left the *Serapis* and moved to block the *Alliance*. The *Serapis* was alone against the three American ships.

The *Bonhomme Richard* chased the *Serapis*. Jones ordered weapons be placed in barrels on the deck—swords, pistols, muskets, and fire grenades. During the chase, the evening turned to night. At seven that evening, Captain Pearson of the *Serapis* shouted to the *Bonhomme Richard*, demanding to know the name and nation of the ship. Instead of answering, Jones had his men fire a cannon toward the *Serapis*.

The moon rose over a glassy sea. The *Serapis* adjusted its sails, moving closer to the *Bonhomme Richard*. Jones raised the American flag and ordered his crew to fire at the *Serapis*—at exactly the moment the *Serapis* fired at the *Bonhomme Richard*. The blast from the *Serapis*'s guns shattered timbers and killed sailors on the deck of the *Bonhomme Richard*.

Unfortunately, two of Jones's largest cannons were old and unsafe—they exploded, killing several of Jones's sailors. The explosions ripped a hole just above the waterline on the starboard side of the ship. Despite this tragedy, the *Bonhomme Richard*'s cannons blasted the deck timbers and rigging of the *Serapis*.

Both ships reloaded and fired again.

"I Have Not Yet Begun to Fight!"

The *Serapis* was faster than the *Bonhomme Richard*, but Jones moved his ship to block the wind, making the *Serapis*'s sails useless. Captain Pearson slowed the *Serapis* and dropped behind Jones's ship—then he ordered his cannons to fire at the tail section of the *Bonhomme Richard*. The blast shattered the rear deck and cabin.

Jones didn't dare fire his biggest cannons and risk more explosions. He had to find a different way to win—and that meant boarding the *Serapis*. Jones ordered the *Bonhomme Richard* closer to the *Serapis*. Captain Pearson tried to move his ship out of Jones's reach—but the *Bonhomme Richard* crunched into the stern of the *Serapis*.

The decks of the two ships were so close that Captain Pearson and Captain Jones could see each other's faces by moonlight. Pearson asked Jones if he was ready to surrender.

Jones laughed and shouted, "I have not yet begun to fight!"

Moments later, the *Serapis* and the *Bonhomme Richard* became tangled together, the rigging of each ship's bow fastened to the other's stern. Captain Pearson knew that Jones intended to board the *Serapis*, so he dropped anchor. He hoped to halt his ship while the *Bonhomme Richard*, under full sail, kept moving forward. This, he hoped, would tear the two ships free from each other.

But Jones's crew had tied the two ships tightly together. Instead of separating, the ships circled each other like a pair of dancers.

With its cannon muzzles pressed up against the *Bonhomme Richard*'s hull, the *Serapis* fired, shredding the American ship's gun decks. Jones and his crew snatched up swords, pistols, and grenades. From the quarterdeck, Jones's gunners aimed smaller cannons down on the *Serapis* and blasted away.

Jones was about to order his crew to board the *Serapis* when he saw British soldiers on the stern, armed with muskets. They were ready to fire on the Americans as soon as they started to cross over to the British ship. Jones knew it would be useless to try boarding through a hailstorm of British musket fire.

Jones ordered his men to cut the lines and separate the ships.

"Let Us Do Our Duty"

As the two ships drifted apart, Jones tried to position his ship to fire at the *Serapis*. But the *Bonhomme Richard*'s rudder was disabled. The ship wallowed helplessly. Seeing that the American ship was stalled, Captain Pearson turned the *Serapis* and slammed his ship into the *Bonhomme Richard* like a battering ram—and the two ships were again locked together.

The collision caused the *Bonhomme Richard*'s flag to fall. The British sailors mistakenly thought the Americans had lowered their flag as a signal of surrender—and they started cheering. An American sailor rushed to raise another flag. Other American sailors fired muskets and pistols at the British sailors. The British sailors stopped cheering and ran for cover.

John Paul Jones seized the moment.

He called to his sailing master, Samuel Stacey, and together they began tying the two ships tightly together with stiff, heavy rope. Jones wanted to make sure the *Serapis* could not get away. As the two men struggled with the rope, Stacey began to use bad language.

Jones said, "Mr. Stacey, it is no time for swearing now. You may the next moment be in eternity. Let us do our duty."

After the sea battle had raged for more than two hours, the *Bonhomme Richard* had few guns capable of firing. The

Serapis had blown so many holes in the American ship's hull that cannonballs whistled through the ship without hitting anything.

Jones and his crew kept fighting. One American sailor named William Hamilton crawled out on a yardarm with a sack of fire grenades. Leaning out over the enemy ship's deck, Hamilton tossed grenades at the open hatches in the deck. One grenade dropped through the hatch and exploded next to sacks of gunpowder. The gunpowder blew up and set off other explosives in a chain reaction of blasts.

The *Bonhomme Richard* was burning and sinking. The American flag had been shot away. From the deck of the *Serapis*, Captain Pearson called to John Paul Jones, demanding surrender.

Jones shouted back, "I am determined to make you strike." (By this he meant, "I am determined to make you lower your flag and surrender.") Jones and his crew fought on.

Captain Pearson realized that, even though the American ship was sinking, Jones was winning the battle. In desperation, he sent a boarding team to take over the American ship—but the Americans met them with guns and swords, driving them back onto the *Serapis*.

Finally, Captain Pearson admitted defeat and offered his surrender. He would later confess that it was the "extraordinary and unheard-of stubbornness" of John Paul Jones that convinced him to surrender. Jones simply would not give up.

Captain Pearson climbed over to the deck of the *Bonhomme Richard* and stood face-to-face with Jones. Without saying a word, he handed his sword to Jones, symbolizing his surrender.

Jones accepted Pearson's sword and said, "Sir, you have defended your ship with credit to yourself and honor to your service."

Captain Jones and his crew worked hard to save the *Bonhomme Richard* by pumping seawater out of the ship, but there was too much damage. For two days, the ship slowly settled into the sea. On the morning of September 25, Jones ordered his crew to leave their ship and board the captured *Serapis*. Then the *Bonhomme Richard* slipped beneath the waves.

In 1780, King Louis XVI honored John Paul Jones with a medal, l'Institution du Mérite Militaire (the Institution of Military Merit). The king also gave Jones the title of Chevalier (Knight). Jones wore the title proudly for the rest of his life. In 1787, the Continental Congress gave Jones a gold medal for courage that read "Chevalier John Paul Jones."

Congress promised Jones a new ship—a seventy-four-gun ship named *America*. But Jones never took command of the ship. The war ended before it was completed, and Congress gave the ship to France to help repay America's war debt.

John Paul Jones died in Paris in 1792. He was buried in a crypt at the Naval Academy in Annapolis, Maryland. History remembers Jones as the "Father of the American Navy." His story reminds us that the key to achieving great goals is a spirit of "extraordinary and unheard-of stubbornness." Whenever we are tempted to surrender, our answer must be, "I have not yet begun to fight!"

17

Sybil Ludington: The Female Paul Revere

Statue of Sybil Ludington on Gleneida Avenue in Carmel, New York, by Anna Hyatt Huntington

In April 1777, a force of two thousand British soldiers landed at Compo Beach near Fairfield, Connecticut. They marched toward the town of Danbury, where the Continental army had stored food, guns, ammunition, and tents. The storehouse was guarded by about two hundred American soldiers. The British Redcoats forced the American troops to surrender, then they raided the storehouse and took all the gunpowder and ammunition.

The Redcoats ran through Danbury, looting and burning the town. While Danbury burned, an American messenger escaped from the city on horseback. He rode toward the home of Colonel Henry Ludington in Fredericksburg, New York.

Sometime after eight that night, the rider reached Colonel Ludington's home. After receiving the terrible news, Colonel Ludington wondered what he should do. He wanted to assemble his militia, but his soldiers were scattered on their farms. How would he get the word to them? He couldn't go himself—he needed to stay home to assemble the militiamen.

Colonel Ludington turned to his daughter Sybil. She had just turned sixteen, but she could ride a horse, and she knew where every member of the militia lived.

Though it was raining and the roads were dangerous at night, Sybil agreed to go. She saddled up her horse and set off down the muddy road with dark woods on either side. Whenever she reached a militiaman's home, she rode up to the house, pounded on the door, and gave the word: "Form up at Colonel Ludington's house, and be ready to fight!"

She may have ridden as far as forty miles that night. Her ride was probably two or three times as long as Paul Revere's ride two years earlier. She rounded up the militia, and by daybreak, the militiamen were all assembled at the Ludington home.

As the militia started off for Danbury, Sybil fell into bed, exhausted.

Ludington's militia joined up with seven hundred Continental army soldiers. The American forces met the British at the village of Ridgefield, Connecticut. Though the Americans were outnumbered, they fired from behind trees and fences, catching the Redcoats by surprise. The British regrouped and forced the Americans backward through the streets of Ridgefield—then they turned and hurried back to their ships at Compo Beach. The Americans chased them and shot at them the whole way.

George Washington later visited Sybil at her home and personally thanked her for her courage and quick action. Sixteen-year-old Sybil Ludington rode alone and called the militia to the battle. She showed us what a young leader looks like.

18

Baron von Steuben: Silk-Robed Warrior

Baron von Steuben at Valley Forge, artist unknown

O n September 11, 1777, the Continental army led by General George Washington suffered a crushing defeat in the Battle of Brandywine. The retreating Americans had to leave the city of Philadelphia undefended. The British captured the city on September 26 and would occupy it for nine months.

On October 4, General Washington's army suffered another defeat at Germantown, Pennsylvania. After the battle,

Washington took his remaining twelve thousand troops to Valley Forge. There they spent the winter.

Washington's men were exhausted from long battles, and they were low on food and short of blankets. Most soldiers had no shoes. They tied rags around their feet to keep from freezing. Many soldiers died of disease or of the cold. Most of the soldiers had lost hope.

General Washington knew he was losing the war. He blamed himself because he did not have a military education. He had learned military tactics years earlier while fighting in the French and Indian Wars. But there was much he didn't know. He wondered why his men were getting sick all the time. Instead of growing stronger at Valley Forge, his men were steadily becoming weaker. Washington didn't know what to do—and he worried that his army might starve to death or quit fighting.

But help was on the way. On December 1, 1777, a ship docked in Portsmouth, New Hampshire. A military officer from the German kingdom of Prussia stepped off the ship and onto the wharf. His name was Friedrich Wilhelm Ludolf Gerhard Augustin von Steuben.

George Washington had never heard of von Steuben, and he didn't know that this Prussian officer was on his way to Valley Forge. The arrival of Friedrich von Steuben would change the course of the Revolutionary War.

Sleigh Bells and Silk

Friedrich von Steuben joined the army of Prussia at age seventeen. He served so well that he became an assistant to King Frederick the Great. He studied the military arts in King Frederick's school of war, which trained the most feared military leaders in the world.

He left the Prussian army in 1763 when he was thirty-three years old and took a job as an assistant to a German prince. The job didn't pay well, but it allowed von Steuben to use the title of Baron. From then on, he called himself Baron von Steuben.

He wanted to make a lot of money, so he tried to get a position with a foreign army. One of his friends was the French minister of war. The French minister gave von Steuben's name to the American ambassador in Paris, Benjamin Franklin.

While reading the French minister's letter of recommendation, Franklin misunderstood one detail. The letter said (in French) that von Steuben had served as a captain in the army of Prussia. Franklin misunderstood, and he thought that von Steuben had served as a general—a much higher rank. So Ben Franklin wrote a letter to General Washington, urging him to hire "General von Steuben" as a military advisor.

When Benjamin Franklin met Baron von Steuben, he gave him the letter of introduction. The baron was to hand the letter to General Washington in person. Franklin also gave von Steuben the money he needed to travel to America.

Baron von Steuben hired four men as assistants and had special uniforms designed for himself and his men. Unfortunately, von Steuben made the mistake of having the uniforms made of red cloth—the same color the British Redcoats wore. On December 1, 1777, when he and his assistants stepped off the ship in Portsmouth, New Hampshire, the Americans almost arrested them as British soldiers.

On February 5, 1778, von Steuben arrived in York, Pennsylvania, where the Continental Congress was meeting after the British captured Philadelphia. The baron expected the Continental Congress to give him and his assistants a large salary. He didn't know that Congress was out of money. He was disappointed when Congress offered to pay him only after America had won the Revolutionary War. It wasn't the offer he had hoped for, but he accepted it.

Two weeks later, Baron von Steuben arrived at Valley Forge. General Washington and his cold, poorly dressed men were shocked when they saw him. Baron von Steuben rode into the camp in a shiny sleigh fitted with twenty-four jingling bells. He wore a silk robe trimmed in white fur. On his lap was a miniature greyhound named Azor, who went everywhere with him. His four assistants also rode in the sleigh.

When von Steuben stepped out of the sleigh, everyone could see that he was a tall man—as tall as General Washington himself—and he looked like a man of confidence and strength. One of Washington's soldiers later said that he looked like a "fabled god of war."

Big Changes at Valley Forge

When Baron von Steuben walked around the camp at Valley Forge, he was horrified. He immediately understood why the American soldiers were always getting sick. He made changes throughout the camp to improve the health of the soldiers.

In those days, there were no bathrooms with toilets that flushed or sewer pipes to carry waste. Instead, the soldiers used a hole in the ground, or a trench called a latrine. At Valley Forge, the latrines were close to the kitchen tents and the water supply, which caused disease germs from the latrines to spread to the food and water that the soldiers ate and drank.

Baron von Steuben completely changed the camp. He moved all the kitchen tents and water barrels to one end of the camp. He moved the latrines far away on the other side of the camp. As soon as von Steuben made these changes, the soldiers stopped getting sick.

Next, von Steuben began a training program for the soldiers. He wrote out military instructions in German, and his secretary would translate the instructions into French. Then Washington's secretary translated the French into English.

Under von Steuben's direction, Washington's top assistants Colonel Alexander Hamilton and General Nathanael Greene wrote an army manual—a book of rules and instructions for soldiers. The book was called *Regulations for the Order and Discipline of the Troops of the United States.* General Washington had the book given out to soldiers throughout the Continental army. Many of its instructions are still used by the US military today.

Baron von Steuben trained the Americans in the best traditions of the armies of Europe. He taught them how to march, shoot, and fight with bayonets. He showed them a faster way to fire and reload their guns. He chose the best soldiers to go out and train the soldiers at other army camps throughout the Thirteen Colonies.

General Washington was amazed at the change in his troops. On May 5, 1778, at General Washington's request, Congress appointed Baron von Steuben Inspector General of the Continental army with the rank and pay of a major general.

Baron von Steuben spoke only German, and he spoke to the soldiers through interpreters. His speech and mannerisms, his elegant uniform, and his forceful personality impressed and inspired the troops.

Warriors and Winners

On July 16, 1779, American soldiers led by General "Mad Anthony" Wayne attacked the British at Stony Point, New York. The raid took place under the cover of darkness. The Americans, all trained by Baron von Steuben, were armed with bayonets on their unloaded muskets. No one fired a musket. The Americans carried out the surprise attack in total silence.

The military operation was a complete success. The Americans drove the British out of the highlands overlooking the Hudson River. The mission was successful because of Baron von Steuben's bayonet training.

In the final years of the war, von Steuben served as General Washington's chief of staff, and they remained friends after the war. Baron von Steuben attended President Washington's first inauguration in New York City in 1789.

At the end of the war, Congress was slow in paying von Steuben the money he was promised. But he had made many wealthy friends during the war, and they helped him buy land in New York.

Baron von Steuben earned the respect and admiration of his soldiers. They knew he cared about their lives and their health—and he cared about winning the war as much as they did. Though he was firm and strict, the soldiers trusted him and admired him because he turned them into warriors—and winners.

19

Nathanael Greene: Warrior with a Limp

Engraving of Nathanael Greene from *The Biographical Cyclopedia of Representative Men of Rhode Island*

Few Americans know about Nathanael Greene's role in the Revolutionary War. But if he had not served in the war, America might not have won the Revolution.

Nathanael Greene was born to a wealthy Quaker family in Warwick, Rhode Island, in 1742. The Quakers of

Greene's time were people who followed the Bible, especially the teachings of Jesus, and who refused to take part in war.

Though Greene was raised in the Quaker faith, he didn't think that it's always wrong to go to war. He believed that people sometimes had to fight against injustice. He also believed that British rule was unjust and had to be opposed—even if it meant war.

When Greene was a boy, he fell and injured his knee. For the rest of his life, he walked with a limp. He also suffered from asthma (which sometimes made it hard for him to breathe) and poor vision in his right eye.

Like many great leaders, Greene loved books and spent much of his free time reading. As a young man, he spent as much money as he could on new books. He loved reading about military history.

However, his interest in the military made his Quaker family and fellow church members unhappy. After he attended a military parade in 1774, church leaders told him he could no longer be a part of the Quaker fellowship.

A Self-Taught Soldier

In 1774, Nathanael Greene married Catharine Littlefield. That same year, he helped establish a Rhode Island militia called the Kentish Guards.

The Revolutionary War began in April 1775, when the British attacked Lexington and Concord, Massachusetts. The Rhode Island legislature made Greene a general in the army of Rhode Island. Later, in 1775, he became a general in the newly formed Continental army, where he served alongside General George Washington.

It was hard for Greene and his young wife to be separated from each other, so Catharine often visited him at the army camp.

Nathanael Greene was a self-taught soldier. Most of his military education came from books. But he soon gained frontline experience, leading men into battle at Massachusetts, New York, and Pennsylvania.

In 1778, during the terrible winter at Valley Forge, General Washington gave Greene the job of quartermaster general of the Continental army. Instead of leading men into battle, Greene ran an army camp. He kept track of supplies and tried to keep the soldiers fed and paid (though there was never enough food or money). He hated the job, but he was willing to do whatever Washington asked of him.

In February 1779, the arrival of Baron von Steuben brought many changes to Valley Forge. Nathanael Greene helped von Steuben write the training manual for the Continental army. He learned a lot about military training and tactics by watching von Steuben train the soldiers during their time at Valley Forge.

A New Kind of War

By 1780, the Revolutionary War was going badly in the southern states. The British captured Charleston, South Carolina, on May 12. Three months later, on August 16, American forces suffered a terrible loss at the Battle of Camden, South Carolina. In that battle, General Horatio

Gates (who was a poor leader and a coward) commanded 2,500 American militiamen who faced a much smaller force of 800 British troops, commanded by General Charles Cornwallis.

General Gates had not trained his forces to fight. He sent his troops to the battlefield while he stayed far behind, where it was safe. When Cornwallis's well-trained troops advanced with bayonets on their muskets, all 2,500 American militiamen threw down their guns without firing a shot. Then they ran from the battlefield.

One of Gates's officers, General Edward Stevens, tried to get the Americans to stand and fight, but they all ran in panic. General Stevens later described the disaster in a letter to the governor of Virginia, Thomas Jefferson: "Picture it as bad as you possibly can, and it will not be as bad as it really is."

The British chased the retreating Americans for more than twenty miles and took almost half of them as prisoners. When General Gates heard that his troops ran from the battlefield, he jumped on his horse and rode north as fast as he could. By nightfall, he was sixty miles away, in North Carolina. Some in the Continental army wanted to put General Gates on trial for cowardice. Though he was never put on trial, he was removed from command.

General Washington chose his trusted friend from Rhode Island, General Nathanael Greene, to take command of American troops in the South.

After working at a desk job for two years, General Greene welcomed the chance to lead soldiers into battle. He had a plan for defeating Britain's General Cornwallis. He was going to fight a new kind of war—an approach to fighting that the British had never seen before.

Guerrilla Warriors

The British approach to war was simple. Their troops would march out onto the battlefield in their bright red uniforms and form two lines—the first line kneeling, the second line standing behind them. On command, they would fire their weapons. Then they would reload and shoot again.

Greene's new kind of war was "guerrilla warfare." *Guerrilla* was originally a Spanish word that meant "raiding team," from the Spanish word for war *guerra*. General Greene trained his troops to travel in small, fast-moving raiding teams. He taught them how to catch the British troops by surprise, to attack quickly, then vanish into the woods.

Greene's goal was to wear the British down. He avoided facing Cornwallis's troops on an open battlefield. British troops would march in ranks down the main roads. Greene taught his troops to sneak through swamps and forests, where a large army couldn't go. Then they would strike before the British knew what hit them.

When General Greene took command of the southern forces in December 1780, British troops controlled large parts of South Carolina and Georgia. General Cornwallis had increased his army to 6,000 soldiers. General Greene had only 1,600 soldiers, and many of them were battle-weary and discouraged.

General Greene divided his forces into two groups. He took command of the main force of one thousand soldiers.

He gave General Daniel Morgan command of the smaller six-hundred-man force.

General Morgan understood this new kind of warfare. He trained his troops to hide in the woods and use surprise attacks. He showed them how to trick the enemy into chasing the Americans into a trap the Americans had laid out for them. But General Greene told Morgan that, for now, he should not attack the British army. Morgan's men needed rest.

Morgan disobeyed General Greene's orders. He came up with his own plan to trap a British force led by Lieutenant Colonel Banastre "Bloody Ban" Tarleton. He planned to attack the Redcoats near a little town called Cowpens, South Carolina. He placed his best marksmen in the woods. When Tarleton's soldiers marched into view, the marksmen took a few shots, hit a few British soldiers, then ran away. Tarleton's Redcoats ran after them.

Morgan's marksmen would shoot, then run away, shoot, then run away. The Redcoats kept chasing them—right into Morgan's trap. Suddenly, one thousand British foot and horse-mounted soldiers found themselves in a clearing surrounded by woods—where Morgan's men, all six hundred of them, had the British surrounded. Morgan's soldiers opened fire, and the Redcoats had nowhere to go.

When the smoke cleared, more than eight hundred of Tarleton's Redcoats were killed, wounded, or captured. Tarleton escaped with only two hundred of his troops. General Morgan had disobeyed General Greene's orders, but he had used Greene's tactics to defeat the British at the Battle of Cowpens.

It was such a huge American victory that General Nathanael Greene forgave Morgan for disobeying orders.

Setting a Trap for Cornwallis

After the Battle of Cowpens, General Greene joined up with Morgan's forces. Together, they led their forces in a retreat toward North Carolina. They were following the same plan that Morgan had used to defeat Tarleton: retreat and trick the enemy into following them. They hoped to trick General Charles Cornwallis into following them to North Carolina, far from his supplies of food and ammunition.

While Greene's main force retreated north, he sent a smaller group of guerrilla fighters to attack Cornwallis's troops. The guerrilla fighters hid behind trees and rocks, attacked suddenly, then vanished into the woods. Cornwallis had never seen such tactics before, and he couldn't understand. He thought the Americans were cowards for not standing on an open battlefield and fighting the traditional way.

Meanwhile, as General Greene took his main force to the north, he was studying maps, looking for a place to stand and fight Cornwallis. He needed a place where the Americans would have the advantage. On February 22, 1781, Greene led his troops across the Dan River into North Carolina. Soon, General Cornwallis would follow him into a trap.

By early March, Greene had received reinforcements from Virginia and North Carolina. He now had four thousand troops, and they were rested, well-trained, and ready to face the Redcoats.

On March 14, Greene's army made camp at Guilford Courthouse, North Carolina (the town would later be named Greensboro in honor of Nathanael Greene). This was the battlefield Greene chose—the place where the Americans had the advantage.

General Greene set up three defensive lines. The first and second lines were manned by militiamen. The third line was manned by Continental army soldiers who had been well-trained in Baron von Steuben's "Prussian Exercise." Greene had a plan to fool the British.

On the afternoon of March 15, 1781, General Cornwallis ordered an all-out attack against the Americans. As the British charged the first line, the militiamen fired at the British—then they turned and ran away. The British thought the Americans were fleeing in panic, but they were following General Greene's brilliant plan.

Next, the British attacked the second line of militia. These militiamen fired at the British—then they turned and ran away. Again, they were following General Greene's plan.

The Redcoats kept moving forward, right into General Greene's trap. Cornwallis ordered an attack against the third line of Continental army soldiers—but these soldiers didn't run. They fought furiously.

The shocked and surprised British troops ran away from the American soldiers. Cornwallis ordered his Redcoats to attack again—but this time they were attacked by American cavalry soldiers on horseback, led by General "Light-Horse Harry" Lee.

General Cornwallis couldn't believe his eyes. A bunch of uncivilized backwoodsmen (that's how he thought of the

Americans) were beating the best-trained army in the world! How could this happen?

Cornwallis ordered his cannons to fire at the Americans—but the Americans and British soldiers were all fighting in one place. When the British cannons roared, as many British soldiers were killed as Americans.

General Greene saw that his army was outnumbered, and he ordered a retreat. The Battle of Guilford Courthouse was over. General Greene had lost the battle. However, the British had lost so many soldiers and the Americans so few that General Greene had actually won by losing. He had made the American army stronger by retreating from the battlefield.

The Battle of Cowpens and the Battle of Guilford Courthouse caused terrible losses among the British forces. Because the Americans were beating the British, the British found that they couldn't get Loyalist Americans to join the British army anymore.

General Cornwallis later wrote, "Greene is as dangerous as Washington. He is vigilant, enterprising, and full of resources. There is but little hope of gaining an advantage over him. I never feel secure when encamped in his neighborhood."

General Nathanael Greene became known as the "Fighting Quaker." At the end of the Revolutionary War, he limped home to a hero's welcome in Rhode Island. He taught American soldiers how to fight and win—even by retreating. He described his new way of winning wars as "We fight, get beat, rise, and fight again."

20

Peter Francisco: A One-Man Army

US Stamp honoring Peter Francisco, artist unknown

Few people have heard the story of Peter Francisco. But it's one of the most amazing stories of the Revolutionary War.

Peter Francisco came to the Virginia Colony from the European nation of Portugal. He was sixteen years old when he joined the American army in 1776. Though he was young, he was big for his age, standing six and a half feet tall. He had the strength of a bodybuilder because he had worked for years in a blacksmith shop.

In the fall of 1777, Peter fought in the Battle of Brandywine and the Battle of Germantown in Pennsylvania. He suffered wounds at Germantown that forced him to stay in bed for weeks at George Washington's army camp in Valley Forge. In June 1778, at the Battle of Monmouth, New Jersey, he was shot in the right thigh. The wound would never fully heal. Even though he later fought in many battles, he always had pain in his right leg.

Peter fought under the leadership of General "Mad Anthony" Wayne at the nighttime Battle of Stony Point, New York, in July 1779. He was the second American to climb over the British defenses and enter the fort. He fought the Redcoats at close range, and one British bayonet slashed a nine-inch-long gash across his stomach. Though he was bleeding, he continued fighting and tore down the flag of Great Britain. Then he raised the American flag over the captured fort. General Wayne reported Peter's brave actions to General Washington.

The Soldier with a Sword

Peter Francisco often went into battle with a six-foot-long broadsword strapped to his side. He fought at the Battle of Camden under the cowardly General Horatio Gates. While most of the Americans retreated in panic, Peter showed amazing courage. He saw an American cannon that was stuck in the mud. He didn't want the British to capture it, so he fought his way forward, lifted the cannon barrel on his shoulder, and carried it off the battlefield. The British won the battle, but Peter saved the American cannon.

In March 1781, Peter fought under General Nathanael Greene in the Battle of Guilford Courthouse, North Carolina.

He was wounded in the leg by a British bayonet. His commanding officer sent him home to Virginia to recover from his wounds.

In July, while Peter was in Virginia near a place called Ward's Tavern, he ran into a band of eleven British raiders. The raiders served under Lieutenant Colonel Banastre "Bloody Ban" Tarleton. They had survived the Battle of Cowpens six months earlier. They hated the Americans, and they were looking for a fight. The leader of the British raiders wanted the silver buckles on Peter's shoes. He told Peter to bend down and take the buckles off.

Peter had no sword or gun—and he was outnumbered eleven to one. He raised his hands as if to surrender. One of the soldiers, who had a sword strapped to his side, bent down to take the silver buckles. In a flash, Peter grabbed the man's sword from its scabbard and struck him on the head.

Now, with sword in hand, he swung the blade at the British soldiers. One fired his musket, hitting Peter in the side—but the bullet passed through his skin without doing serious harm. Another soldier, seated on a horse, tried to shoot at Peter, but his musket failed to fire.

Reaching up, Peter grabbed the horseman's musket and yanked the man out of his saddle. Then he leaped up on the horse and rode away.

The Hercules of American Independence

Peter rested at home, then he joined General Washington's army at Yorktown, Virginia, in October. He was present with

Washington when General Cornwallis surrendered and the Revolutionary War came to an end.

Today, a monument to Peter Francisco stands in New Bedford, Massachusetts. The words on the monument read:

In Honor of Peter Francisco
The Hercules of American Independence
"Without him we would have lost two crucial battles, perhaps the war, and with it, our freedom.
He was truly a one-man army."
General George Washington

21

Marquis de Lafayette: The Youngest General

First Meeting of Washington and Lafayette by Currier and Ives

When the Marquis de Lafayette first arrived in America from France, he had no battle experience—none. He was only nineteen years old. But when he introduced himself to General George Washington, he told Washington that Congress had made him a general in the Continental army.

At first, Washington couldn't believe it. This young Frenchman—a general? He thought Lafayette was going to be nothing but trouble. Soon, however, Lafayette became one of Washington's closest friends and most trusted generals.

The Marquis de Lafayette was born in France in 1757. His full name was Marie Joseph Paul Yves Roche Gilbert du Motier, Marquis de Lafayette. The title "marquis" is French for "ruler of a border area." A marquis is a French nobleman.

Lafayette was two years old when his father was killed in battle by the British. He grew up hating the British for what they'd done. His mother died when he was thirteen, and he was raised by his grandmother.

In 1771, the thirteen-year-old Lafayette began his military training by marching in parades. When he was sixteen, he was made a lieutenant in the mounted infantry. One of his fellow soldiers told him that the Revolutionary War had begun in America. Lafayette was excited to hear about the people in America rising up to fight the British. He decided to join the American cause.

Lafayette's Hero, George Washington

Lafayette went to King Louis XVI and asked for the king's blessing to go to America and fight for the glory of France. The king told him that France was not fighting for America. This war was between America and Great Britain. He ordered Lafayette to remain in France.

But Lafayette wanted nothing more than to fight the British—even if he had to disobey the king of France. He met with an American diplomat named Silas Deane and said that he wanted to fight for America. Deane liked Lafayette and wrote a letter of introduction for him. The letter urged Congress to make Lafayette a general in the American army. Deane didn't realize that Lafayette had no battlefield experience.

Lafayette sailed to America, arriving in June 1777. He traveled to Philadelphia with the letter from Silas Deane in his pocket. He gave the letter to the Continental Congress, and Congress gave him the rank of general in the Continental army.

Lafayette heard that his hero, General George Washington, was having dinner with other military officers in a tavern in nearby Chester, Pennsylvania. Lafayette went to the tavern to meet Washington. He walked in and saw his hero, standing taller and more impressive than anyone else in the room. Washington symbolized everything Lafayette wanted to be—a man of dignity, honor, and bravery.

At first, Washington was happy to meet Lafayette, the keen young Frenchman who was eager to fight in the war. But when Washington learned that Congress had given Lafayette the rank of general, he was horrified. Did Congress *really* expect General Washington to let a teenager lead soldiers into battle?

Lafayette followed Washington around, watching everything his hero did. Washington knew that Lafayette took his rank seriously and expected to command American troops. Finally, a letter arrived from Paris. It was signed by Silas Deane and Benjamin Franklin. The letter urged Washington to give Lafayette a minor job on the battlefield.

Lafayette's chance to face the enemy would soon come.

The Battle of Brandywine

In August and September 1777, about seventeen thousand British troops marched toward Philadelphia. Washington believed the British would cross the Brandywine River at Chadds Ford, so he put most of his troops there. He sent Lafayette with a small force of soldiers to a place north of Chadds Ford. He thought the Marquis de Lafayette would be safe there.

Washington didn't know that more than half of the British troops were going to the very spot where Lafayette would be. Instead of sending the young Frenchman out of danger, Washington had sent him into the thick of the battle.

When the British attacked, Lafayette was on the front lines. Musket balls zipped dangerously close to his head. One musket ball passed through his lower left leg. Ignoring the pain, Lafayette continued fighting. He soon grew weak from loss of blood and had to be helped onto his horse. Reluctantly, he left the battlefield—but he had won the admiration of the American soldiers who had fought at his side.

The Battle of Brandywine was a bitter loss for the Americans. It led to the British capture of Philadelphia. But it was Lafayette's first taste of battle—and he had fought bravely.

General Washington wrote a report on the Battle of Brandywine, naming the Marquis de Lafayette as a hero of the battle. The report was printed in newspapers throughout the Thirteen Colonies. Lafayette became famous from Massachusetts in the north to Georgia in the south.

After the Battle of Brandywine, Washington and Lafayette were close friends for life.

Lafayette's "Punishment"

Lafayette remained with Washington at Valley Forge during the harsh winter. He made many friends there, including Baron von Steuben, Nathanael Greene, and Alexander Hamilton. As his English improved, Lafayette began to understand American politics better. When he was in France, he had thought that *all* Americans believed in freedom and hated British rule. He was shocked to learn that many Americans were Loyalists who supported King George III.

In June 1778, General Washington sent General Charles Lee, with the help of the Marquis de Lafayette, to lead an attack against the British at Monmouth Courthouse, New Jersey. General Lee was a poorly prepared military officer. He gave confusing orders to his troops, and the soldiers didn't know where to go or what to do.

Lafayette saw the American attack falling apart. He sent a rider on a fast horse to deliver an urgent message to General Washington, begging Washington to come and take command. Washington came and found that his forces were losing the battle.

Washington removed General Lee from command. Then he organized his soldiers to attack the British again. Under his leadership, the attack succeeded. The British fled the battlefield.

Washington thanked Lafayette, for if the message had not gotten to Washington in time, the battle would have been lost.

In January 1779, with Washington's permission, Lafayette went home to France. He planned to return to America in a few months and continue the fight.

Yet, Lafayette was worried about going home to France. King Louis XVI had forbidden him to go to America—and Lafayette had disobeyed. When Lafayette's ship docked in France, soldiers arrested him. But instead of taking him to prison, the soldiers took him to a luxury hotel. He spent eight days under arrest in the hotel—then the king ordered that he be set free.

The king had been angry with Lafayette for disobeying and going to America. But the king knew that Lafayette was now a hero in both America and France. He had brought glory and honor to the French nation. Though he felt he had to "punish" Lafayette, he sent him to a luxury hotel instead of prison. Lafayette was relieved to know that the king was proud of him.

In March 1780, Lafayette left France and sailed to Boston. Crowds of cheering people lined the streets and welcomed him back to America. But Lafayette was saddened to learn that the American war effort was going badly. The British were winning battle after battle, and the Americans were losing the war.

The Battle of Yorktown

Lafayette arrived at Washington's camp at Morristown, New Jersey, in May 1780. It was a happy reunion for both men. General Washington was glad when Lafayette told him that France was sending a large military force to America.

Washington gave Lafayette command of the Virginia Continental forces. In August, Lafayette led his troops to Yorktown, Virginia, where the British troops of General Cornwallis occupied the city. By September, seventeen thousand American and French troops, led by General George Washington and General Jean-Baptiste Rochambeau of France, joined Lafayette and surrounded Yorktown.

General Cornwallis and his Redcoats were trapped In Yorktown. They were running out of food and ammunition.

On October 14, two small American forces, one led by the Marquis de Lafayette and the other by Alexander Hamilton, captured two of the ten small British forts (called "redoubts") that surrounded Yorktown. The capture of these two small forts left Yorktown open to attack.

General Cornwallis ordered his troops to attack the Americans and fight their way out of the city. But the British troops were hungry, discouraged, and outnumbered. The American and French troops easily forced them back.

Finally, General Cornwallis knew he had to accept defeat. On October 19, he surrendered his eight thousand soldiers to General Washington.

The Battle of Yorktown was the last major land battle of the Revolution. It would take nearly two years for a peace treaty to be signed between Great Britain and the United States. But the Revolutionary War was over.

Lafayette was a hero to the American people. The United States Congress honored Lafayette, making him an honorary US citizen.

He was happy that America had won. But he was heartbroken over having to leave his great American friend. He

wrote to George Washington, "Goodbye, my dear General
. . . I assure you that my love, my respect, my gratitude for
you, are above expression." He sailed from Boston on December 21, 1781.

The Hero of Two Worlds

The Marquis de Lafayette returned to France as a conquering hero. His nation gave him the rank of major general in the French army. He returned home to his family's large estate, where he raised wheat and other crops.

What kind of man was Lafayette? He was brave, honorable, and generous. Two years after he returned to France, the wheat harvest failed across much of the country. Many people were going hungry because there was too little wheat to buy. But Lafayette's farm had produced a great harvest of wheat.

The manager of Lafayette's farm knew that many wheat farmers were raising their prices sky-high to cash in on the wheat shortage. He told Lafayette he should raise his prices and sell his wheat for a huge profit as well. Lafayette knew the poor people of France couldn't afford higher prices, so he told his manager he would not sell his wheat at a higher price. Instead, he said, "This is a time to give." And he gave his wheat to the poor for free.

Lafayette was a man who believed in freedom, fairness, and kindness. He was loved by the people of America and the people of France. That is why he became known as *Le Héros des Deux Mondes*, "The Hero of the Two Worlds."

22

The Fighting Women of the Revolution

Molly Pitcher at the Battle of Monmouth, engraver
unknown, based on a painting by Charles Yardley
Turner

Not enough has been written about the fighting women
of the Revolutionary War. Some fought as soldiers, disguised as men. Some were spies and message carriers.
Some risked musket fire and cannon blasts to carry pitchers
of water to thirsty soldiers. Here are some stories of the
brave women of the Revolutionary War.

Close Call with a Cannonball

Mary Hays of New Jersey was thirty years old when the Revolution began. During the harsh winter of 1777, she joined her husband William at General Washington's camp at Valley Forge. She washed clothes and blankets and took care of sick soldiers.

Her husband was trained by Baron von Steuben to fire cannons. During battles, she would carry water to her husband and the other soldiers. Some of the water she carried was for the soldiers to drink. She also carried water to clean the barrels of the cannons.

Every time the cannon was fired, the gun barrel had to be mopped with wet sheepskin to remove soot and cinders. This meant the cannon crews needed a lot of water. That water was carried in pitchers by other women like Mary as well. The women who carried water became known as "Molly Pitchers."

Mary Hays went with her husband in the summer of 1778 to the battlefield at Monmouth Courthouse in New Jersey. At eight in the morning on June 28, 1778, the Americans attacked the British forces. By half past ten, the Americans were losing the battle.

The weather was hot and miserable. Many soldiers, both British and American, collapsed from heat stroke. Mary's husband William fell unconscious because of the heat. She watched the soldiers carry him off the battlefield. Then she stepped up and took William's place. She loaded the cannon, as she had seen William do, then fired a cannon blast at the British.

As she stood behind the cannon to reload, a British cannonball whooshed between her legs. It ripped away the lower part of her dress. She looked down at her torn dress and saw that she wasn't hurt. Then she calmly loaded and fired the cannon once more.

Mary continued loading and firing the cannon until darkness fell and all the shooting stopped. She thought she would have to fight again the next morning. But when the sun came up, the Redcoats were gone. They had retreated during the night.

William Hays got well and continued to serve on the cannon crew. Mary continued serving as a "Molly Pitcher." General Washington personally thanked Mary Hays for her bravery on the battlefield.

Husband-and-Wife Soldiers

The first woman to serve in the American army was Anna Marie Lane of Virginia. When she was in her early twenties, she cut her hair and disguised herself as a man. Then she went with her husband, John Lane, to join the Continental army.

From 1776 to 1781, John and Anna fought side by side in many battles in New York, New Jersey, Pennsylvania, and Georgia. Anna fought in the Battle of Germantown, near Philadelphia, on October 3, 1777. She was shot in the leg and wouldn't let the doctors take care of her. She was afraid the doctors would find out she was a woman. Her injury made it hard for her to walk, yet she continued to fight in the war.

After the war ended in 1781, John and Anna Marie Lane settled on a farm in Virginia. Anna also volunteered at a military hospital, caring for soldiers. In 1808, the state of Virginia gave Anna money to live on to thank her for her bravery as a soldier in the Revolutionary War.

No Doctors for Deborah

Deborah Sampson of Plympton, Massachusetts, was another woman who disguised herself as a man to join the army. She never knew her parents. She was raised by a widow who taught her to read. When the widow died, she became a servant to a wealthy family.

When she was twenty-one, she cut her hair, put on men's clothes, and tried to join the Continental army. She called herself "Timothy Thayer." But someone recognized her and told the commander that "Timothy" was a woman. The commander sent her away.

A few weeks later, Deborah went to another town and tried to join the army again. This time, she called herself "Robert Shirtliff." She was placed in an infantry company and trained to be an expert marksman. She fought in several battles.

Deborah Sampson sometimes led teams of soldiers on dangerous missions. She even dug trenches. One time, she helped capture fifteen enemy soldiers.

In June 1782, she was hit in the forehead by a bullet. The bullet left a gash in the skin of her forehead, but she kept fighting.

A month later, she was shot twice in the upper leg in a battle near Tarrytown, New York. She didn't want the doctors to find out she was a woman, so she did surgery on herself. She used a knife to remove one of the musket balls. She couldn't reach the other musket ball—it was in too deep. She sewed up the skin with a needle and thread.

Deborah Sampson came down with an illness in September 1783. The doctor discovered that "Robert Shirtliff" was a woman. He took Deborah to his house, where his wife and daughters helped nurse her back to health.

When Deborah Sampson was well, the doctor gave her a sealed note to give to her commanding officer. Deborah delivered the note to the general. The note told the general that "Robert" was a woman. The general was kind to Deborah. He told her she couldn't stay in the army, but he gave her money to pay for her journey home to Massachusetts.

In 1802, Deborah Sampson traveled from town to town, giving talks about her service as a woman in the army. In 1804, her friend Paul Revere convinced Congress to give her a monthly income because of her brave service in the war.

The Guardian of the Bridge

Prudence Wright was thirty-five years old when the Revolutionary War began. She lived in the village of Pepperell, Massachusetts. Though she supported the Revolution, her brothers Thomas and Samuel were Loyalists who spied for the British.

In April 1775, Prudence overheard her brother Thomas making secret plans with another Loyalist spy named

Leonard Whiting. The two men were going to take a message to the British, telling them where Patriot weapons and gunpowder were hidden.

Prudence told other women in the village about the spies. That night, the women picked up wooden clubs, iron pans, and pitchforks. They headed to the bridge at the edge of town. They had lanterns for light, but when they reached the bridge, they covered their lanterns and waited in the dark.

After a while, the women heard two riders coming on horseback. One was Prudence's brother Thomas. The other was Leonard Whiting.

Prudence stepped forward, uncovered her lantern, and shone the light at the two surprised men. "Stop!" she commanded. "Get down from those horses!"

The other women came out of the darkness and surrounded the men.

Thomas turned his horse around and rode off, nearly trampling one of the women.

Leonard Whiting didn't think the women would really try to stop him, so he spurred his horse forward. The women leapt at him, dragged him from his horse, and threw him on the ground.

They searched him and found papers hidden in his boot. They were the plans showing where the Patriot weapons and gunpowder were stored.

The women pulled Whiting to his feet and marched him to a nearby tavern. They held him prisoner that night. In the morning, they handed him over to the Patriot militia.

Because of her leadership and bravery, Prudence became known as the "Guardian of the Bridge."

The Sorrow of Captain Molly

Margaret Cochran Corbin served in the war as a nurse and cook. She traveled to the battlefield with her husband, John Corbin, who fired cannons.

On November 16, 1776, John was one of six hundred American soldiers defending Fort Washington on Manhattan Island. The fort was surrounded by four thousand British troops. Margaret was one of the few women in the fort, helping to supply the gun crews with water and gunpowder. Many of the soldiers called her "Captain Molly" out of respect for her bravery.

The fort was defended by only two cannons. While John was loading one of the cannons, he was shot by the enemy. Margaret was standing close by and watched him fall dead.

Though she was stricken with sorrow, she had no time for grieving. She stepped up and took her husband's place. She loaded and fired the cannon again and again. After hours of fighting, she was hit by gunfire. She fell to the ground, wounded in her left arm, her chest, and her jaw.

The British stormed the fort and won the Battle of Fort Washington. Margaret Cochran Corbin was in prison for a few days, then the British released her because of her wounds. "Captain Molly" was never able to use her left arm again, but she recovered from her other wounds. For many years, she remained heart broken over the death of her husband John.

The Song of Soldier Sally

Sally St. Clair was another woman who disguised herself as a man to join the army. She was the daughter of African and French parents and was born in South Carolina.

She served for a while in the militia of Francis Marion (who was nicknamed the "Swamp Fox"). She fought bravely but died at the Battle of Savannah in 1779. Only after her death did her fellow soldiers find out she was a woman.

Some stories claimed Sally was in love with one of her fellow soldiers. She was killed, the stories say, when she stepped in front of a British spear that was aimed at the soldier she loved. Whether the stories were true or not, they were told and retold—and Sally St. Clair became an American legend.

George Pope Morris wrote a poem called "Sally St. Clair: A Song of Marion's Men." In the poem, Sally disguises herself so well that even the man she loves doesn't recognize her:

> In the ranks of Marion's band,
> Through morass and wooded land,
> Over beach of yellow sand,
>   Mountain, plain and valley;
> A southern maid, in all her pride,
> March'd gayly at her lover's side,
>   In such disguise
>   That e'en his eyes
> Did not discover Sally.

We owe our American liberty and independence to the women of the Revolution. They never thought of their own safety but fought bravely for freedom. When a male soldier fell, a woman would stand up, take his place, and finish the job. These women would fight. They would sacrifice. Sometimes they would die.

They were women who loved America, and they were leaders.

23

Alexander Hamilton: He Wanted to Fight

Scene at the Signing of the Constitution of the United States by Howard Chandler Christy. George Washington stands at the desk near the flags on the wall.

There's a picture of Alexander Hamilton on the ten-dollar bill. He received this honor as one of America's most famous Founding Fathers. (The Founding Fathers were the people who served in the Revolution and helped design the government of the new American nation.)

Hamilton served bravely in the Revolution and was one of General Washington's favorite commanders. After the Revolutionary War, Hamilton urged Congress to adopt the United States Constitution. He designed America's money system. He even started a major newspaper, the *New York Post*, which is still published today.

We don't know the exact year Alexander Hamilton was born, but it was between 1755 and 1757. He was born on the tiny island of Nevis in the British West Indies.

Hamilton's father abandoned his family in 1765. His mother, Rachel, died from a tropical fever when Hamilton was just

Detail from the painting by Howard Chandler Christy, showing Alexander Hamilton leaning toward Benjamin Franklin

twelve or thirteen. Thomas Stevens, a wealthy merchant in Nevis, gave the boy a foster home. The house was filled with books, and young Hamilton read constantly. He was eager to learn about the world.

When Hamilton was a teenager, he wrote a letter describing a terrifying hurricane. His description of the hurricane was so vivid and exciting that it was published in an American magazine. The people of Nevis were proud of young Hamilton's writing. They collected money to send him to college in America.

Arriving in America

Hamilton came to America in October 1772, and he enrolled at King's College in New York City in the fall of 1773. In college, he wrote essays in favor of a revolution against Great Britain. After the start of the Revolutionary War, Hamilton joined a voluntary militia.

He did his militia training in the morning before his classes. By studying military history and tactics from books, Hamilton soon became a leader in the militia.

While he was a student in college, he led a raid to capture British cannons at the lower end of Manhattan Island. A British ship roared its cannons at them, but Hamilton and his militiamen seized the cannons and hauled them away. No militiaman was killed or injured.

The Battle of Long Island began on August 22, 1776. The thunder of cannons echoed across New York City. Five days later, 32,000 British troops, 30 warships, and 170 troop-transport ships arrived in New York.

General Washington's army had to escape from the city. The British took over New York and would control the city for seven years. King's College was forced to close. Alexander Hamilton escaped from the city and formed a sixty-man unit called the New York Provincial Company of Artillery.

Hamilton led his soldiers in battle in New York and New Jersey. Though he was only twenty years old, he was so successful that General George Washington offered him a job on his staff.

A Broken Relationship

Alexander Hamilton served as Washington's top assistant for four years. He learned how Washington thought, planned strategy, and led the troops. Hamilton's ability to speak French enabled him to translate conversations with the Marquis de Lafayette while the young French general was learning English.

In 1780, Hamilton married Elizabeth Schuyler. He called her Eliza, and they were very much in love. Though Hamilton was newly married, he wanted to get back to the battlefield and lead troops again. He felt that writing the general's letters and sitting in strategy meetings was a waste of his time and talent. He wanted to *fight*.

When Hamilton was twenty-six years old, a misunderstanding damaged his friendship with Washington. Hamilton was unhappy because Washington wouldn't send him to the battlefield.

But General Washington didn't even know his assistant was unhappy. He had problems of his own. The war was going badly. Some of his soldiers had rebelled against his leadership. Washington was in a sour, impatient mood.

One day in February 1781, Washington was walking up the stairs of his headquarters. At the same time, Hamilton was walking down the stairs with a paper in his hands. As they passed each other, Washington said, "I wish to speak with you."

Hamilton nodded and went downstairs to hand the paper to the Marquis de Lafayette. He stopped to talk to Lafayette for a minute or two. Then he went back upstairs.

General Washington was waiting for him—and he was angry.

"Colonel Hamilton," Washington said sharply, "you have kept me waiting for ten minutes! I must tell you, sir, you treat me with disrespect."

Hamilton thought it had been only two minutes, not ten. He said, "I am not conscious of any disrespect, sir—but since you think it necessary to tell me so, I'm leaving the army."

Washington said, "Very well, sir, if that is your choice."

Alexander Hamilton walked away.

General Washington later felt sorry that he had scolded Hamilton. He sent his friend a message, saying he was sorry for his sharp words.

But Hamilton was still angry, even after Washington's apology. He stood by his decision and resigned from the army.

Hamilton and Lafayette at Yorktown

Even though he had left the army, Alexander Hamilton still wanted to lead troops into battle. Five months after resigning, he wrote to General Washington and told him he wanted to command troops in battle. Washington sent a message back to Hamilton, saying he would give him a command.

By this time, Washington had turned his attention to the coastal city of Yorktown, Virginia. The forces of the great British General Charles Cornwallis occupied Yorktown. Washington believed that if he could defeat Cornwallis at Yorktown, the war would be over.

Washington offered Alexander Hamilton command of one thousand soldiers from New York and Connecticut. He also placed the Marquis de Lafayette in command of seven thousand American troops. Washington sent Hamilton and Lafayette to Yorktown with instructions to keep Cornwallis trapped inside the city.

Hamilton was happy to lead troops again—and to rejoin his good friend Lafayette. Both men were eager to begin the battle that would end the war.

Meanwhile, General Washington joined forces with French General Jean-Baptiste Rochambeau. The two generals commanded a combined force of seventeen thousand American and French troops. They began their journey to Yorktown to join up with Lafayette and Alexander Hamilton.

On the night of October 14, 1781, Hamilton and Lafayette each assembled a team of their best three hundred men. It was a moonless night. They planned to attack two small forts (called "redoubts") that were part of the British defensive line around Yorktown. The soldiers attached their bayonets but left their muskets unloaded. They needed to attack in total silence, so they had to make sure that no one fired his gun by accident and alerted the British.

Hamilton signaled his men. They scrambled out of their trenches and ran toward one small fort, a quarter of a mile away. The first line of soldiers quickly tore down a barrier of sharpened wooden stakes. This allowed the next line of Hamilton's soldiers to rush up to the fort. One soldier knelt when he reached the wall of the fort. Another soldier climbed onto the kneeling soldier and leapt up onto the wall.

Alexander Hamilton was one of the first men to climb over the wall and enter the fort. He and his men worked in silence—and they completely surprised the enemy. Working quietly, they used their bayonets on the first few Redcoats—and the other Redcoats dropped their guns and surrendered.

It took less than ten minutes for Hamilton's men to capture the fort. Lafayette's men quickly captured the other fort. The mission had gone perfectly—a complete success.

When the sun came up, General Cornwallis saw that two of the small forts that defended Yorktown had been captured. Yorktown was defenseless against a full-scale invasion. On October 19, Cornwallis surrendered. The Revolutionary War was over.

Afterward, Lafayette wrote a report on the Yorktown mission—and his report was full of praise for Alexander Hamilton's courage and leadership. Lafayette's report was published in newspapers throughout the United States. Hamilton became a national hero.

A Leader of Vision

After his triumph at Yorktown, Hamilton returned to New York. His wife Eliza gave birth to a son named Philip on January 22, 1782. Philip was the first of eight Hamilton children.

Alexander Hamilton purchased law books, studied hard, and became a lawyer in October 1782. Because of his fame as a war hero, he was chosen in 1787 as a delegate for the national convention in Philadelphia. He wrote up a plan for a strong federal government.

Two other delegates to the convention, James Madison and John Jay, used some of his ideas in writing the

Constitution of the United States. Madison, Jay, and Hamilton published a series of essays explaining the new Constitution. Those essays became known as *The Federalist Papers*.

In 1789, George Washington was elected president of the United States. He chose Hamilton as the nation's first secretary of the treasury. Hamilton helped design the government of the United States. He planned how the money system would work and how to keep the government from going into debt.

In 1795, Alexander Hamilton resigned from the government. He returned to being a lawyer in New York City.

For several years, Hamilton had been bitterly feuding with Vice President Aaron Burr. At sunrise on July 11, 1804, the two men stood on a grassy meadow near Weehawken, New Jersey. Burr had challenged Hamilton to a duel. Hamilton had accepted the challenge.

The two men faced each other. Hamilton fired first. He believed in the tradition of wasting his first shot, so he aimed his pistol at a tree. Aaron Burr had never heard of the tradition of wasting the first shot, so he took deadly aim and fired.

As the crack of the gunshot still echoed through the trees, Alexander Hamilton crumpled to the ground.

His horrified friends picked him up and lifted him into a carriage. Then they drove him to a house a few miles away. A doctor came to care for him, but Hamilton said weakly, "This is a mortal wound, Doctor." He died the next day with his wife and children at his side.

Alexander Hamilton fought bravely in the Revolutionary War. He helped design the government of the United States. He was an American leader who helped change the world.

24

Betsy Ross: Maker of Flying Colors

The Birth of Old Glory by Edward Percy Moran

Betsy Ross was born on New Year's Day, 1752, in New Jersey. Her parents named her Elizabeth, but they soon shortened her name to Betsy. When Betsy was three years old, her parents, Samuel and Rebecca Griscom, moved to Philadelphia.

The Griscom family belonged to the Quaker faith. They believed in the Bible and the teachings of Jesus—and they hated wars and fighting. Betsy's parents taught her that when she was old enough to marry, she should marry a peaceful man of the Quaker faith.

After she finished school, Betsy worked in a shop that made items out of cloth, such as bedcovers, curtains, and tablecloths. She learned how to sew and repair clothing. While working in the shop, she fell in love with a man who also worked there. His name was John Ross.

Betsy's parents didn't approve of John because he was not a Quaker. He attended Christ Church in Philadelphia, which belonged to the Church of England.

On November 4, 1773, Betsy and John went to Gloucester, New Jersey, without telling Betsy's parents. They were married there, then they returned to Philadelphia and opened their own sewing and repair shop.

Betsy's husband knew many people who would soon play important roles in the American Revolution. John's uncle George Ross was a lawyer, an officer in the Pennsylvania militia, and a political leader. He would later become one of the signers of the Declaration of Independence.

Uncle George introduced John and Betsy to a wealthy Pennsylvania merchant, Robert Morris (he would also later sign the Declaration of Independence). Uncle George also introduced them to General George Washington. In 1774, John and Betsy Ross made a set of bed curtains for General Washington's bed.

In 1775, after John and Betsy had been married for less than three years, John died. There is no record of how he died. He probably came down with smallpox or another disease. Betsy was just twenty-four years old and a widow. Though she was heartbroken and lonely, she continued to run the sewing business by herself.

Two months after the Battles of Lexington and Concord in April 1775, the Second Continental Congress formed the Continental army. The Revolutionary War had begun—and Betsy was soon busy sewing army tents, uniforms, and flags.

According to a story that was passed down to Betsy Ross's grandchildren, Betsy received a great honor in May or June 1776. That's when George Washington was in Philadelphia to accept his appointment as commander in chief of the Continental army. Betsy received three visitors at her sewing shop—Uncle George Ross, Robert Morris, and General George Washington.

General Washington asked Betsy if she would do a favor for her nation. Would she sew a flag for the United States of America?

The Continental Congress had chosen a design for the flag. It would have thirteen red and white stripes with a blue field in the corner with thirteen white stars. Washington asked that the stars each have six points. Betsy suggested a five-pointed star instead. It could be made by simply folding a piece of white cloth and making a single snip of the scissors.

Washington, Morris, and Ross agreed to Betsy's suggestion. Betsy then sewed the first American flag.

Some historians wonder whether Betsy Ross really made the first American flag. They say there are no documents to prove whether she did or not.

The story of Betsy Ross and the first American flag has been told and retold by Betsy's grandchildren and great-grandchildren. We can't prove that it's true, but we do know that Betsy Ross knew General Washington very well. So it's certainly possible.

I think the story of Betsy Ross is true. I believe she really was the first maker of America's flying colors, the Red, White, and Blue.

What do *you* think?

25

George Washington: Father of His Country

General George Washington Resigning His Commission by John Trumbull

There have been many stories told about George Washington that are not true. You may have heard when young George was a boy, he chopped down his father's cherry tree. According to the story, his father asked him about the tree, and George said, "I cannot tell a lie. I did it with my little hatchet."

This story was made up by a man named Mason Weems for a book he wrote in 1809. He wanted to honor George Washington. But you can't really honor someone by making up false stories.

What's the *true* story of George Washington's life? The truth is much more exciting than any made-up stories.

Washington's Rules

George Washington was born in Virginia on February 22, 1732. He grew up on Ferry Farm near Fredericksburg.

By the time Washington was sixteen, he had copied with pen and ink a little book of 110 rules for living. These rules were first written down in 1595 by priests in France. The language of Washington's time can be hard to understand today.

"Let your discourse with men of business be short and comprehensive."
In other words, speak simply, and don't use many words.

"Use no reproachful language against any one; neither curse nor revile."
Be respectful, and don't use bad language.

"In all causes of passion admit reason to govern."

If someone argues with you, stay calm, and try to get
   along.

"Be not curious to know the affairs of others."
Mind your own business.

"Speak not evil of the absent for it is unjust."
Don't say bad things about people behind their backs.

When George Washington was a teenager, he wanted to
be a good man and leader. He was not a perfect man—and
he knew it. But he set a goal of being as good as he could
be. Every day, he tried to improve his character.

What kind of man was George Washington? He was brave.
He refused to surrender. He was humble—he never acted
like he was better than other people. He cared about his
soldiers. Though he was not a perfect man, he loved God,
and he loved his country.

Battle-Tested Character

In 1752, the government of Virginia put twenty-year-old
Major George Washington in charge of a militia group. He
went to the Ohio Valley and made peace with the Iroquois
people. He talked to the French and tried to get them to
leave the Ohio Valley. The French commander refused to
leave, but he respected Major Washington. Because of
Washington's bravery and skill, the Virginian government
gave him a promotion.

Two years later, Lieutenant Colonel George Washington led forty men in an attack on a French-controlled fort. The battle lasted less than fifteen minutes before the French surrendered. Later, Washington wrote to his brother John, "I heard the bullets whistle, and, believe me, there is something charming in the sound."

In 1754, his book *The Journal of Major George Washington* was published in Williamsburg, Virginia, and London. The book made Washington famous throughout the Thirteen Colonies and Great Britain.

In July 1755, Washington was with British General Edward Braddock on a mission to force the French out of the Ohio Valley. General Braddock's soldiers were attacked by French soldiers and Native American warriors. Braddock was shot in the chest.

Lieutenant Colonel Washington bravely organized his troops as the bullets flew around him. He helped rescue General Braddock from the battlefield. As the British general was dying, he gave Washington the sash he wore over his uniform. Washington later wore that sash as commander in chief of the Continental army.

In 1758, after leading troops in more than twenty battles, Washington retired from the military. He married Martha Dandridge Custis, a twenty-eight-year-old widow. They settled at his Mount Vernon estate. George Washington expected to spend the rest of his life as a farmer in Virginia. But the world was about to change—and Washington's life would change too.

Retreat, Escape, but Never Surrender

The Battles of Lexington and Concord took place on April 19, 1775. The Revolutionary War had begun.

Two months later, Congress created the Continental army and chose George Washington as commander in chief. Washington humbly said, "I do not think myself equal to the command I am honored with."

He accepted the job because every member of Congress voted for him. The delegates chose Washington because he was famous for always telling the truth and keeping his promises.

Congress offered to pay him, but Washington refused the money. He went to work, bringing the various state militias together into a unified Continental army.

His first job as commander in chief was to take charge of the American forces surrounding Boston. As Washington rode on horseback to Boston, crowds lined the streets and cheered for him. He arrived at the outskirts of Boston on July 2, 1775—two weeks after the Americans were defeated at Bunker Hill and Breed's Hill.

Washington met with his troops. He found them poorly trained but eager to fight. He began training them for the battles to come.

The British controlled the city of Boston. They wanted to move out and take control of the rest of Massachusetts. But the Americans kept the British boxed in.

In November 1775, Washington sent twenty-five-year-old Henry Knox to New York. Two months later, Knox returned with cannons the Americans had captured from the British.

After Knox's men placed the cannons on Dorchester Heights at the south end of Boston, the British knew they had to leave. They loaded their troops on ships and sailed out of the city.

After capturing Boston without firing a shot, Washington suffered several defeats. During the Revolutionary War, Washington lost more battles than he won.

Though he had to retreat many times, Washington never surrendered. If a battle went badly, he always had an escape plan. He made sure that his men could retreat, then return to fight another day.

The Invisible Enemy

Soon after the Revolutionary War began, George Washington faced an invisible enemy. That enemy's name was smallpox. We don't have to worry about smallpox today. Modern medicines wiped out the smallpox virus during the 1970s.

In Washington's time, however, people feared this terrible disease. The smallpox epidemic of 1775 to 1782 may have killed ten times as many people as were killed in battle.

Doctors had discovered a way to help people avoid getting smallpox. They would take a small amount of diseased material (such as a scab) from a sick person. Doctors would rub this diseased material on a small scratch in a person's skin. This would cause a very mild form of smallpox that would protect the person from getting a bad case.

This way of protecting people from smallpox was called "variolation." It saved many lives—but it was risky. A few people who were treated this way caught a bad case of the disease and died.

By 1777, smallpox was spreading among the American troops, and many were dying. General Washington had to decide whether to treat his soldiers with variolation. What if the British found out that his soldiers were sick from the treatment? What if they attacked and wiped out his army?

But the disease had already killed many soldiers. Battle plans had been delayed because too many soldiers were sick. The fear of smallpox kept many men from joining the army.

Washington made his decision. He ordered his soldiers to be treated with variolation. His plan was carried out in secret. For weeks, many soldiers were too weak to fight.

The British never learned that American soldiers had been treated. Washington's plan was a complete success. The Continental army became a healthy, strong fighting force because General Washington made the right decision.

The Battle of Long Island

After the British left Boston, Washington took the Continental army to New York City on Manhattan Island. He wanted to keep the British from invading the city. He had his soldiers place cannons and strengthen the defensive walls.

British ships arrived in July and August. They brought a force of more than thirty-two thousand soldiers. On August 22, 1776, the British attacked Washington's main force on Manhattan Island. Many American soldiers were killed or wounded.

Washington had to move his soldiers across the East River to Long Island. They made their camp at Brooklyn Heights.

The British expected Washington to stay in Brooklyn Heights and fight hard. But Washington knew his forces were outnumbered. It would be hopeless to keep fighting. He decided to escape before the British knew they were gone.

A heavy rain fell the afternoon of August 28. Washington ordered his cannons to fire on the British troops as night fell.

Meanwhile, he had his men line up boats on the shore. He ordered most of his troops to walk in silence to the shore. No one spoke. No one lit a lantern. They made their way silently through the rainy night.

Washington had a few soldiers build dozens of campfires up on the heights, where the British could see them. To the British, it looked like thousands of troops were camped on the heights—but the soldiers were all gone.

The escape didn't go as quickly as Washington had hoped. He wanted all nine thousand of his troops off the island by sunrise. But when morning came, the American troops and equipment were still being loaded onto boats. Washington feared that the British could strike at any moment.

Then, unexpectedly, a thick fog rolled in. Washington hoped that the British couldn't see his soldiers in the fog. He continued to help load his men onto the boats.

Meanwhile, British soldiers climbed up to the heights and found the campfires—but no soldiers. The Americans had vanished.

Down on the shore, the last American soldier stepped aboard the last boat. That soldier's name was George

Washington. He refused to leave until all his soldiers were safe.

God protected George Washington and his troops. The fog that hid the Americans from the British eyes was a miracle.

General Washington had lost New York, but his soldiers lived to fight another day.

Losses and Retreats

After the escape from New York, Washington's army suffered a series of losses.

The Americans were forced to retreat from the Battle of Brandywine in Pennsylvania, September 11, 1777. The retreating Americans left Philadelphia undefended. At that time, Philadelphia was the capital of the United States.

When the British entered the city without firing a shot, they cheered and celebrated. They thought the war was over—and they had won. In European wars, when an army captured the enemy's capital, the invaders won the war.

But the Americans didn't play by the rules of old Europe. The Continental Congress had left Philadelphia and moved to the town of Lancaster. The British were not used to fighting an enemy that could pack up the whole government and move down the road.

On October 4, Washington's Continental army launched a surprise attack on the British camp at Germantown, Pennsylvania. He divided his forces into four groups. He wanted them to attack the British at the same time from four directions. Unfortunately, two of the groups got lost in the fog and shot at each other, thinking they were attacking the British. It was a disaster—and the Americans had to retreat.

General Washington learned a lesson. After the defeat at Germantown, he always made his battle plans simple and easy for his troops to follow.

Washington had lost New York. He had lost Philadelphia. He had suffered defeats and retreats at Brandywine and Germantown.

As winter of late 1777 began, the Revolutionary War was at a standstill. Washington led his army of eleven thousand men to Valley Forge, north of Philadelphia. There they would wait for the warmth of springtime and better fighting weather.

During the freezing winter at Valley Forge, Washington's soldiers were hungry and cold. Many became sick and some died. Others simply walked away from the camp and went home.

Washington wrote many letters to Congress. He asked for food, clothing, and blankets for his troops. But Congress told Washington to send his soldiers out to steal food from nearby farmers. Many of those farmers were Loyalists who sold food to the British, so why not steal from them?

But Washington refused to steal. He believed that stealing was always wrong, even if it would help win the war.

Washington led the Continental army for eight years. Finally, he led his troops to the battle at Yorktown, Virginia.

At Yorktown, Washington gathered his finest military minds—heroes we have been reading about in this book. There was Henry Knox, Washington's brilliant young expert on cannons. He pounded the British defenses with cannonballs. Washington's young friends Alexander Hamilton and the Marquis de Lafayette were there, leading the attacks on the two small forts outside the city. Baron von Steuben and "Mad Anthony" Wayne placed troops around the edges of the city, making sure the British couldn't escape.

Finally, on October 19, 1781, General Charles Cornwallis surrendered to General Washington. The Revolutionary War was over.

A Secret Plan to Take over the Government

George Washington continued to serve as commander in chief of the Continental army after the fighting ended. He wrote to Congress, asking for the pay the government owed to his soldiers. But Congress said there was no money to pay them.

Washington's troops were furious. They hadn't been paid in months.

In March 1783, Washington learned that a small number of army officers were planning to attack Congress and take over the government. As the officers began their meeting, General Washington walked into the room. Everyone in the room was shocked. They all wondered if he was going to have them arrested.

General Washington walked to the front of the room and looked at the faces of his men. Then he asked them to be patient and to stop anyone who wanted to take over the government.

He took a letter from his pocket that had been written by a member of Congress. He couldn't read it, so he took out a pair of glasses and put them on. His men had never seen him wearing glasses before.

"Gentlemen," he said, "you will permit me to put on my spectacles. For I have not only grown gray but almost blind in the service of my country."

As Washington read the letter, the officers choked back tears. They remembered all that Washington had sacrificed so that America could be free.

This ended the plan to attack Congress. The officers remained loyal to the United States of America. Weeks later, Congress began paying the soldiers what it had promised.

On September 3, 1783, Great Britain and the United States signed an agreement called the Treaty of Paris. Great Britain accepted the United States as an independent nation.

After leading the Continental army for more than eight years, Washington was ready to go home. On December 4, 1783, he said goodbye to his loyal officers at Fraunces Tavern in New York. Then he returned to his home at Mount Vernon, Virginia, planning to live out his days as a farmer.

Washington's One Great Flaw

I have to tell you about Washington's one great flaw. It's sad but true: George Washington owned slaves. In those days, human slavery had been carried on in many countries for thousands of years. Many people considered it perfectly normal to own slaves.

Though Washington owned slaves, he was troubled about slavery. In a letter to his friend Robert Morris, Washington wrote, "There is not a man living who wishes more sincerely than I do to see a plan adopted for the abolition of [slavery]." He went on to say that a law should be passed to end slavery—and that he would gladly vote for such a law.

Washington wrote to another friend, John Francis Mercer, "I never mean to possess another slave by purchase." He added that he wished that slavery could be ended in America.

Like Thomas Jefferson, Washington was a slave owner who came to believe that slavery was morally wrong. He stopped buying slaves. But what about the slaves he already owned? In his will, he set one slave free upon his death. He arranged for more than a hundred slaves to be freed after his wife's death.

But if he believed slavery was wrong, shouldn't he have set them free while he was alive? Yes, he should have.

Maybe, like Thomas Jefferson, he felt he would be ruined financially if he didn't have slaves to work on his farm. But I believe he should have freed his slaves anyway.

From the time he was a teenager, George Washington tried to improve his character. He tried to be an example for others to follow. Imagine what a difference he would have made if he had freed his slaves. And imagine if he had urged all the farmers and landowners in Virginia to free their slaves.

George Washington was a great leader. He was not a perfect man, but he tried to be a good man. In almost every way you can think of, he *was* a good man.

But he knew that slavery was wrong—and he did not set his slaves free. That was George Washington's great flaw.

A President, Not a King

The leaders of the new American nation had to decide what kind of government they would have. Some said that America needed a completely new kind of government in which the people had a voice. The people should choose their own leaders. If the people thought the taxes were too high or the laws were unfair, they could speak up—and the government would listen.

But there were some who wanted America to have a government just like Great Britain's, with a king to rule the people.

In May 1782, army colonel Lewis Nicola wrote a letter to George Washington. He said that the people were not wise enough to choose their own leaders. Letting people vote for their leaders would lead to an unstable nation where people were always arguing and fighting. Colonel Nicola told Washington that America needed a king. He and some of his army friends would help George Washington become America's "King George."

Washington was horrified when he read Colonel Nicola's letter. He hated the idea of replacing Britain's King George III with a new "King George." He told Colonel Nicola, "Banish these thoughts from your mind." He urged the colonel to never discuss this idea with anyone.

George Washington's humble character helped make America what it is today.

In 1789, Washington was elected the first president of the United States. He invented most of the customs and traditions that US presidents follow today. To make sure the president would never be treated like a king, he asked that people call him simply "Mr. President."

After two terms as president, Washington stepped down from office and went home to his farm at Mount Vernon. King George III of England was amazed that Washington didn't try to rule America like a king. King George admired President Washington and called him "the greatest character of the age."

George Washington died on December 14, 1799. At his funeral, Henry "Light-Horse Harry" Lee, who had served in the Revolution, talked about the kind of man Washington was: "To the memory of the Man, first in war, first in peace, and first in the hearts of his countrymen."

26

We Need Heroes Again

Spirit of '76 by Archibald Willard

The United States of America is a miracle.

Throughout the war, American soldiers were low on food, clothing, shoes, guns, and gunpowder. They were low on everything except courage and a will to win.

The Continental army lost battle after battle. Yet, miraculously, the Americans won the war.

Who were the American soldiers? Most of them were poorly trained farmers and shopkeepers. They faced the army and navy of the most powerful empire in the world—Great Britain. Again and again, the cause for liberty hung by a thread.

But whenever the new nation needed a hero, a leader stepped up and faced the challenge. Some were young women like Sybil Ludington and Emily Geiger, who bravely rode the dangerous roads at night to complete their vital missions. Some were young men like Andrew Jackson, who ignored bullets and cannonballs to carry messages to the battlefield. Some were Black former slaves like Crispus Attucks and Austin Dabney. Some were women like Mary Hays and Deborah Sampson, who faced cannon fire and musket fire for the cause of freedom.

Many young people became great leaders. Twenty-five-year-old Boston bookseller Henry Knox showed the army how to aim and fire its cannons. Young Scottish sea captain John Paul Jones became an American hero—and the British navy's worst nightmare. A young Frenchman without any battlefield experience known as the Marquis de Lafayette became one of Washington's favorite generals.

From the defeat at Lexington to the victory at Yorktown, American heroes had to stand up and face danger for the sake of liberty. Every hero sacrificed greatly to make freedom ring.

America didn't just happen. America was a miracle of God. If you look at the story of the Revolutionary War, you can see the invisible hand of God inspiring great ideas of freedom, raising up heroes, and changing the world.

And America still needs heroes. America needs young leaders who will step up and face the challenges of the twenty-first century.

I'm not saying that America is a perfect nation. I'm not saying that the heroes of the Revolutionary War were perfect people. They weren't. Some, sadly, owned slaves. But the ideas they fought for—the ideas in the Declaration of Independence, the belief that all people are created equal—would eventually end slavery in America.

What does it take to be a hero? You don't have to be perfect. You just have to be willing to do whatever you can. You just need to be ready to step up and face any challenge.

Whenever you see a person being bullied, speak up. Whenever you see people being attacked because they are different from other people, defend them. Whenever you see someone doing wrong, step up and do the right thing. Whenever you hear someone spreading false or mistaken ideas about America, speak up and declare the truth.

You can make a difference in your school, your city, your world. You can be an example to the people around you.

And yes—

You can be a *hero*.

Sources and Suggested Reading

Books for Young Readers

Marsha Amstel and Ellen Beier, *Sybil Ludington's Midnight Ride* (Minneapolis: Millbrook Press, 2000).

Alice Dalgliesh, *The Fourth of July Story* (New York: Aladdin, 1995).

Burke Davis, *Black Heroes of the American Revolution* (New York: Harcourt, 1992).

Ester Forbes, *Johnny Tremain* (New York: Houghton Mifflin Harcourt, 1943, 2011).

Russell Freedman, *The Boston Tea Party* (New York: Holiday House, 2013).

Jean Fritz, *Can't You Make Them Behave, King George?* (New York: Putnam, 1996).

Joe Giorello, *Great Battles for Boys: The American Revolution* (Wheelhouse Publishing, 2022).

Beatrice Gormley, *Friends of Liberty* (Grand Rapids: Eerdmans, 2013).

Kathleen Krull and Anna DiVito, *A Kids' Guide to the American Revolution* (New York: Harper, 2018).

Wil Mara, *If You Were a Kid During the American Revolution* (New York: Children's Press, 2016).

Peter Marshall, David Manuel, and Anna Wilson Fishel, *The Light and the Glory for Young Readers: 1492–1787* (Grand Rapids: Revell, 2011).

Carla Killough McClafferty, *Spies in the American Revolution for Kids* (Emeryville, CA: Rockridge, 2021).

Anne Rockwell, *They Called Her Molly Pitcher* (New York: Dragonfly, 2006).

Rosalyn Schanzer, *George vs. George: The American Revolution as Seen from Both Sides* (New York: National Geographic Kids, 2007).

Clara Ann Simmons, *John Paul Jones: America's Sailor* (Naval Institute Book for Young Readers) (Annapolis, MD: Naval Institute Press, 1997).

Dyana Stan, *Emily Geiger's Dangerous Mission* (New York: Houghton Mifflin Harcourt, 2006).

Lisa Trusiani, *The History of the Constitution: A History Book for New Readers* (Emeryville, CA: Rockridge, 2021).

Graphic Novel Format

Mark Shulman, *Alexander Hamilton: The Fighting Founding Father!* (Show Me History!) (San Diego: Portable Press, 2019).

Mark Shulman, *Benjamin Franklin: Inventor of the Nation!* (Show Me History!) (San Diego: Portable Press, 2020).

Mark Shulman, *George Washington: Soldier and Statesman!* (Show Me History!) (San Diego: Portable Press, 2021).

Selected Sources (Books Written for Adults)

John K. Alexander, *Samuel Adams: America's Revolutionary Politician* (Lanham, MD: Rowman & Littlefield, 2002).

Laura Auricchio, *The Marquis: Lafayette Reconsidered* (New York: Vintage, 2015).

John Buchanan, *The Road to Guilford Courthouse: The American Revolution in the Carolinas* (Hoboken, NJ: Wiley, 1997).

Andrew Burstein, *The Inner Jefferson: Portrait of a Grieving Optimist* (Charlottesville, VA: University of Virginia Press, 1996).

Joseph Callo, *John Paul Jones: America's First Sea Warrior* (Annapolis, MD: Naval Institute Press, 2006).

Ron Chernow, *Alexander Hamilton* (New York: Penguin, 2004).

Joseph J. Ellis, *Revolutionary Summer: The Birth of American Independence* (New York: Vintage, 2014).

Clifton Fadiman and André Bernard, editors, *Bartlett's Book of Anecdotes* (New York: Little, Brown, 2000).

Karin Clafford Farley, *Samuel Adams: Grandfather of His Country* (Austin, TX: Raintree Steck-Vaughn, 1994).

David Hackett Fischer, *Paul Revere's Ride* (New York: Oxford University Press, 1994).

David Hackett Fischer, *Washington's Crossing* (New York: Oxford University Press, 2004).

Thomas Fleming, *Bunker Hill* (Boston: New Word City, 2016).

Benjamin Franklin, *Autobiography of Benjamin Franklin* (New York: Henry Holt, 1916).

Terry Golway, *Washington's General: Nathanael Greene and the Triumph of the American Revolution* (New York: Henry Holt, 2005).

Robert Harvey, *A Few Bloody Noses: The Realities and Mythologies of the American Revolution* (Woodstock, NY: Overlook Press, 2002).

Jerry Holmes, *Thomas Jefferson: A Chronology of His Thoughts* (Lanham, MD: Rowman & Littlefield, 2002).

Joseph Plumb Martin, *The Adventures of a Revolutionary Soldier* (Maine: Hallowell, 1830).

David McCullough, *1776* (New York: Simon and Schuster, 2005).

Thomas Paine, *Common Sense* (Philadelphia: W. & T. Bradford, 1776), Gutenberg.org, June 24, 2017, http://www.gutenberg.org/files/147/147-h/147-h.htm.

Henry S. Randall, *The Life of Thomas Jefferson, Volume 1* (Philadelphia: J. B. Lippincott, 1871).

William Bradford Reed, *The Life of Esther De Berdt: Afterwards Esther Reed of Pennsylvania* (Philadelphia: C. Sherman, 1853).

Evan Thomas, *John Paul Jones: Sailor, Hero, Father of the American Navy* (New York: Simon & Schuster, 2003).

George Otto Trevelyan, *The American Revolution, Vol. I* (New York: Longmans, Green, 1921).

Harlow Giles Unger, *John Hancock: Merchant King and American Patriot* (New York: Wiley, 2000).

William Vincent Wells, *The Life and Public Services of Samuel Adams* (Bedford, MA: Applewood Books, 1865; reprinted 2009).

Pat Williams with Jim Denney, *Revolutionary Leadership: Essential Lessons from the Men and Women of the American Revolution* (Grand Rapids: Revell, 2021).

Gordon S. Wood, *The American Revolution: A History* (New York: Modern Library, 2002).

Selected Sources (Websites)

Central Intelligence Agency, "Intelligence Throughout History: Paul Revere's Midnight Ride," CIA.gov, April 30, 2013, https://www.cia.gov /news-information/featured-story-archive/2010-featured-story-archive /intelligence-history-paul-revere.html.

Jonas Clarke, "Sermon—Battle of Lexington," WallBuilders.com, December 27, 2016, https://wallbuilders.com/sermon-battle-of-lexington -1776/.

Library of Congress, "The American Revolution, 1763–1783: First Shots of War: A Proclamation by British General Thomas Gage, June 12, 1775," LOC.gov, http://www.loc.gov/teachers/classroommaterials /presentationsandactivities/presentations/timeline/amrev/shots /proclaim.html.

Thomas E. Ricks, "The Most Underrated General in American History: Nathaniel Greene?," Foreign Policy, September 22, 2010, https:// foreignpolicy.com/2010/09/22/the-most-underrated-general-in -american-history-nathaniel-greene/.

Image Credits

Image on page 9 is public domain. James Henry Stark, *Stranger's Illustrated Guide to Boston and Its Suburbs*, 1882. Wikimedia Commons contributors, "File:Bostonians Reading the Stamp Act.jpg," *Wikimedia Commons, the free media repository*, https://commons.wikimedia.org/w/index.php?title=Flle:Bostonians_Reading_the_Stamp_Act.jpg&oldid=713024079 (accessed December 21, 2022).

Image on page 13 is public domain. Courtesy of Bridgewater State College Archive, Bridgewater, Massachusetts.

Image on page 17 is public domain. Benson John Lossing, *The Pictorial Field-Book of the Revolution*, 1851, p. 489. https://www.google.com/books/edition/The_Pictorial_Field_book_of_the_Revoluti/MPM_AAAAYAAJ?hl=en&gbpv=1&dq=%22Emily+Geiger%22&pg=PA489&printsec=frontcover.

Image on page 26 is public domain. Wikimedia Commons contributors, "File:Samuel Adams.tif," *Wikimedia Commons, the free media repository*, https://commons.wikimedia.org/w/index.php?title=File:Samuel_Adams.tif&oldid=153008934 (accessed December 21, 2022).

Image on page 33 is public domain. Wikimedia Commons contributors, "File:Boston tea party.jpg," *Wikimedia Commons, the free media repository*, https://commons.wikimedia.org/w/index.php?title=File:Boston_tea_party.jpg&oldid=711747255 (accessed December 21, 2022).

Image on page 37 is public domain. Courtesy of Massachusetts Historical Society.

Image on page 39 is public domain. This version is found on the United States Declaration of Independence, Fascimile on velum, one of 201 produced in 1823 by William J. Stone from a copper plate engraving of the original 1776 manuscript.

Image on page 40 is public domain. Identification of the painter unclear: John Henry Hintermeister and his son Henry Hintermeister used the same signature. Wikimedia Commons contributors, "File:Revere (Paul) arousing Hancock and Adams by Hy Hintermeister.jpg," *Wikimedia Commons, the free media repository*, https://commons.

Pat Williams retired as senior vice president of the NBA's Orlando Magic in 2019 to head up an effort to bring major league baseball to Orlando. He has more than fifty years of professional sports experience and has written more than one hundred books, including the popular *Coach Wooden, Coach Wooden's Greatest Secret, Character Carved in Stone,* and *Revolutionary Leadership.* Find out more at www .patwilliams.com.

Jim Denney is the author of *Walt's Disneyland, Answers to Satisfy the Soul, Writing in Overdrive,* and the Timebenders series for young readers (beginning with *Battle Before Time*). He has written many books with Pat Williams, including *Coach Wooden, The Difference You Make, Revolutionary Leadership,* and *The Sweet Spot for Success.* Learn more at www.writinginoverdrive.com.